Essential Elements for Brand Identity

100 Principles for Designing Logos and Building Brands

Kevin Budelmann
Yang Kim
Curt Wozniak

Rockport Publishers
100 Cummings Center, Suite 406L
Beverly, MA 01915

rockpub.com • rockpaperink.com

First published in the United States of America by
Rockport Publishers, a member of
Quayside Publishing Group
100 Cummings Center
Suite 406-L
Beverly, Massachusetts 01915-6101
Telephone: (978) 282-9590
Fax: (978) 283-2742
www.rockpub.com

Originally found under the following Library of Congress Cataloging-in-Publication Data

Budelmann, Kevin.
Brand identity essentials : 100 principles for designing logos and building brands / Kevin Budelmann and Yang Kim.
p. cm.
Includes index.
ISBN-13: 978-1-59253-578-1
ISBN-10: 1-59253-578-X
1. Logos (Symbols)--Design. 2. Industrial design coordination. I. Kim, Yang, 1968- II. Title. III. Title: 10 principles for designing logos and building brands. IV. Title: One hundred principles for designing logos and building brands.
NC1002.L63B83 2010
741.6--dc22

2010018826
CIP

ISBN-13: 978-1-59253-793-8

10 9 8 7 6 5 4 3 2 1

Design: Yang Kim & Kevin Budelmann

Printed in China

Dedicated to BLT

CONTENTS

Street Trooper
ヤジュウ
Exclusive Tshirts available now
BEAST ヤジュウ

Get
your
Emblem
on.

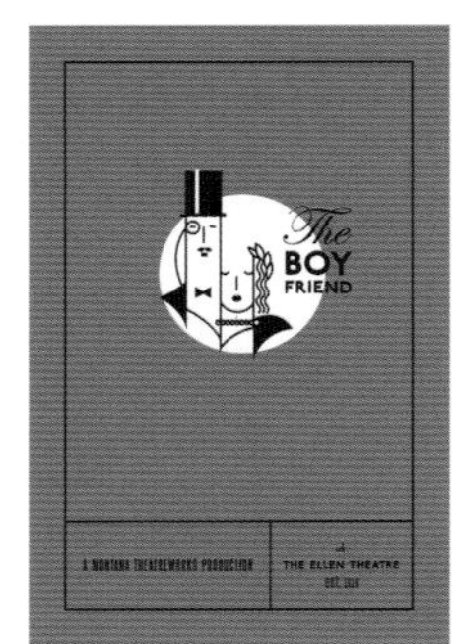
The
BOY
FRIEND

High Glitz
THE EXTRAVAGANT WORLD OF CHILD BEAUTY PAGEANTS

CURZON
75
CELEBRATING
OUR PAST, OUR PRESENT
AND OUR FUTURE

Harvard Design Magazine
Look
Again

DIVAMOTO

Bags

Pfizer

The co-operative
little book of facts
We are
Britain's
most
ethical
brand.*

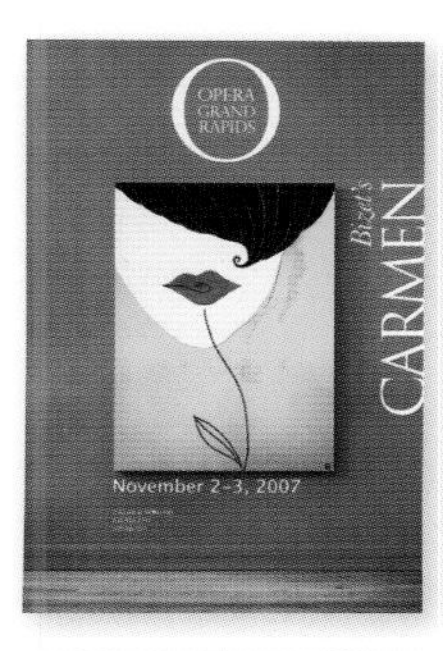
OPERA
GRAND
RAPIDS
Bizet's
CARMEN
November 2–3, 2007

HELLOMOTO

How to look like you have
something intelligent to say.

French
Movie
Channel
Brigitte
Bardot
Weekend:

NEU
FUND
LAND
Wo Möbel fast wie neu sind!

eco

Atelier LaDurance
LES BAUX DE PROVENCE

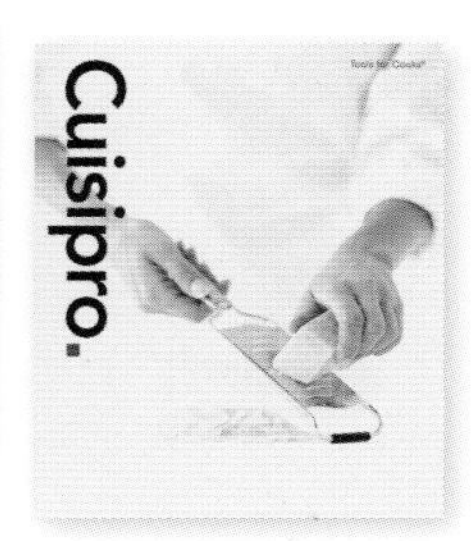
Cuisipro.

Logo

Brand

ROCKPORT

Logos. Brands. What's the Difference?

The name of this book is *Essential Elements for Brand Identity*, but a good portion of it is dedicated to logos. Brands. Identities. Logos. What's the difference?

The word *logo* is short for logotype—a graphic representation of a brand. So, essentially, a logo is a picture that represents the collection of experiences that forms a perception in the mind of those who encounter an organization.

Identity is often (mistakenly) used interchangeably with *logo*, but an organization's identity encompasses much more than its logo. The organization's name is equally as important as the picture used to represent it. Other elements, such as the color of a company's mailing envelopes or the music customers hear while on hold on the telephone, are elements of the identity. Most of the logos we admire more often than not are part of a well-designed system. In such a system, the application of the logo (as well as these other elements) has been as carefully considered as the logo itself.

An exploration of identities without including logos would be like a tour of France without a stop in Paris. Including a discussion of brands and how they relate to identities is like connecting the trip to the culture of Western Europe. It puts it all in context.

It might help to think of it this way: The logo is a picture; the complementary elements and application decisions form a program; and the perception created by the picture and the program form the visual center of the brand.

The structure of the book logically flows from this evolution. We explore each "Essential" as it relates to graphic identity (in a word, logos). Then, we follow some of the logos we dissect through their applications as part of successful identity programs. Finally, we discuss the ways design (and designers) can influence customer perceptions through brand identity.

1 Illustrative Logos

All illustrative logos are pictures, but they cover quite a range of meaning. Some literally illustrate a product or service. Others symbolically represent an idea or metaphor more loosely related to an organization's mission. A third group suggests meaning or captures a spirit rather than illustrating something specific.

The more literal an illustrative logo is, the less work a potential customer needs to do to interpret it. If your client is a dentist, and you create a logo for her practice that resembles a toothbrush, her logo functions like a highway sign. It says, "This is the dentist, not the cobbler."

Sometimes, an illustration can be concrete while its meaning remains abstract. Name your moving company Mayflower Transit, and using a picture of the famous Pilgrim vessel for your graphic identity becomes the obvious choice—provided you can make a connection in the minds of your potential customers between the thing being illustrated and a meaningful aspect of your business.

Apple provides the classic example of an illustrative logo with its meaning left open for interpretation. Apple doesn't sell apples, but you wouldn't know that from its logo—a stylized image of an apple with a bite taken out of it. The company's original logo, with its direct reference to Isaac Newton and the apple tree, was replaced in 1976.

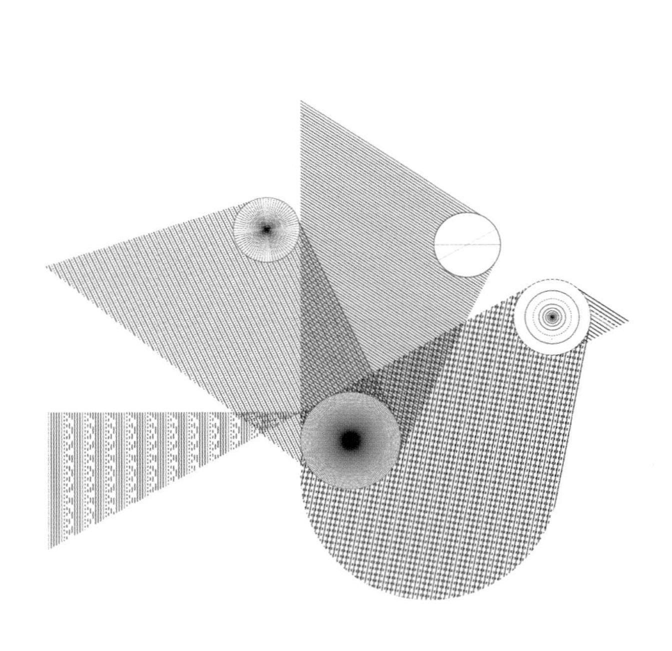

1

2

3

4

5

Some logos literally illustrate the name of an organization, while others represent the product or service being provided. Still others stand for a more abstract idea.

1. Mobile Digital Commons Network
The Luxury of Protest
Michael Longford, Peter Crnokrak

2. Treehouse Records
Juicebox Designs
Jay Smith, Kristi Smith

3. Punane Puu
LOOVVOOL
Hannes Unt, Kadri-Maria Mitt, Valter Kaleta

4. Plaid Owl
Palazzolo Design
Gregg Palazzolo, Ben Benefiel

5. Community Farm of Simsbury
Nordyke Design
John Nordyke

6. artwagen
hopperhewitt
Marcus Hewitt

7. Mayflower Transit
Lippincott
Rodney Abbot, Bogdan Geana, Michael D'Esopo, Sasha Stack

8. The Port of Long Beach
Siegel+Gale
Sven Seger, Marcus Bartlett, Monica Chai

9. Pappy's Smokehouse
TOKY Branding + Design
Eric Thoelke, Dan Klevorn

10. Butler's Pantry
TOKY Branding + Design
Eric Thoelke, Katy Fischer, Elvis Swift

11. Uncle Billy's
Idea 21 Design
Tom Berno, Jeff Davis

12. Bulliard's of Louisiana Pepper Sauce
Britton Design
Patti Britton, John Burgoyne, John Burns

13. Ben Jacob's Plumbing
circle k studio
Julie Keenan

6

7

8

9

10

11

12

13

2 Visual Style

Creating a coherent identity program involves more than slapping a bug on baseball hats and polo shirts. The style of additive visual elements—photography, illustration, etc.—truly helps define an identity program.

Sometimes, designers overlook the obvious. Granted, there's a fine line between obvious and banal, and you do not want to cross it. Keep in mind, however, that art and design serve different purposes. Art is a one-to-one communication. Design needs to communicate directly with a specific group of people. When developing the photography or illustration style for a program, you don't need to trade clarity for sophistication. A lot of programs flounder by using sophisticated, but unclear imagery. Fall into this trap, and you fail to communicate anything.

Insightful use of communicative images reinforces—and in some cases, establishes—a program's visual tone.

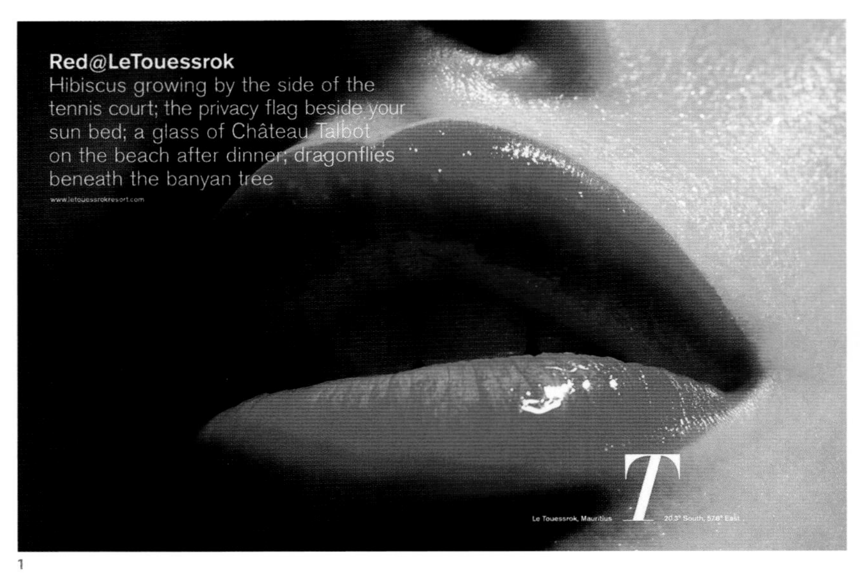

1

2

3

4

1–3. Le Touessrok
Pentagram
John Rushworth, Charlotte Fritzberg, Jess Earle, Graham Montgommery, Jan Baldwin, Karim Illya, Naresh Ramchandani

4. Cinémoi
The Luxury of Protest
Stefan Boublil, Peter Crnokrak, Ekaterina Erschowa

5. 2FRESH LLC
2FRESH

6. Rebel Green
Wink
Richard Boynton, Scott Thares

7. Kresimir Tadija Kapulica
Bunch
Vanja Šolin of Process 15

5

6

7

Color or black-and-white photography, editorial or non-representational illustrations: A strong and clear image style helps define a program aesthetic.

3 An Aesthetic Niche

Images add immediacy, power, and clarity to communications, from stained-glass church windows to Michael Jordan billboards. Consider what images mean for a brand identity, and choose wisely.

The evolution of online stock photography and photo-sharing sites has given designers access to a plethora of easy-to-come-by images. Search iStockphoto for "guys in ties running through airports," and you'll find ample imagery to represent just about any business customer. But using these clichéd images won't carve out a visual niche for the brand. It will merely add to the noise.

With everybody using the same pool of photos, it's hard to use images as a unique differentiator or identifier. In response to this, brand designers need to work harder to create new visual artifacts. Additional creative minds can serve as wonderful collaborators in this effort, lending a new sense of depth and experience. Often, a good photographer or illustrator can work side by side with a design director to carve out a new niche with a level of visual sophistication appropriate for the client.

1

Photographs of flatware taken from dramatic angles add interest and variety to the Gourmet Settings brand website. Heath Ceramics relies heavily on graphic color photography to tell the story of its brand.

1. Gourmet Settings
Hahn Smith Design
Nigel Smith, Alison Hahn

2. Heath Ceramics
Volume Inc.
Adam Brodsley, Eric Heiman, Amber Reed, Christine Leventis, Jeffery Cross, Mark Allen Johnson, Renee Zellweger

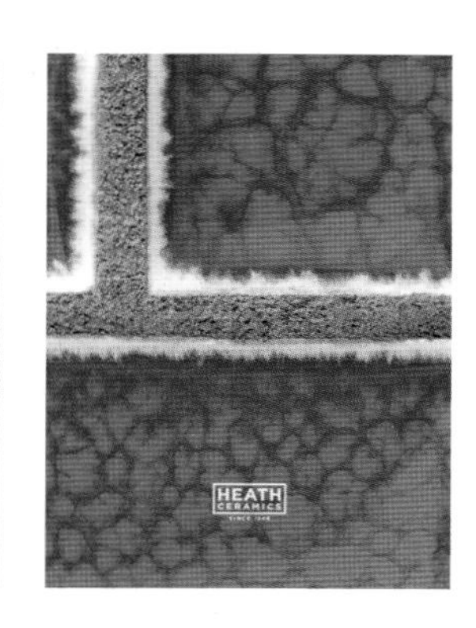

A common modern vision has drawn generations of craftspeople to the Heath family, each one devoted to our heritage of classic design and quality production. The craft and character of the handmade is what we love.

2

4 Color Choices

We could dedicate an entire book to the subject of color—and plenty of people have. As a designer, there's a lot to learn about using color, from the psychology to the science. When developing a graphic identity, however, perhaps the single most important thing to know about color is at what point in the process to make decisions about it.

Color brings such an immediate emotional quality to a mark—it can tempt designers into jumping ahead and designing with a particular color in mind. Resist this temptation. Complete your initial design for each new mark without regard to the color(s) it will eventually take on. Because most graphic identities face color limitations depending on the application, you'll need to ensure that a mark will work in several different colors. And because colors are often influenced by trends, what feels contemporary today may look dated tomorrow.

That said, a color treatment can make or break a graphic identity. Color choices that are too dated, illegible, unsophisticated, etc., can drag down even the most wonderfully drawn mark.

Once you're ready to consider color for a mark, start with the natural dimensions of color: hue (red vs. blue), saturation (bright blue vs. blue gray), and brightness (light blue vs. dark blue). Revisit the color wheel and think about how complementary colors with the same values play visual tricks. Consider additive color (where every color together makes black) or subtractive color (where every color together makes white). Understand the context of color—how a light shape on a dark field looks smaller than a dark shape on a light field.

1. CgB
Carol García del Busto

2. Kink
MINE™
Christopher Simmons, Tim Belonax

3. Americas Team
CAPSULE
Brian Adducci

4. NEUFUNDLAND
Simon & Goetz Design GmbH & Co. KG
DörteFischer, Julia Brett, Heiko Winter

5. Avenue for the Arts
David R. Schofield

6. Garza Architects
Murillo Design, Inc.
Rolando G. Murillo

7. Seven Oaks
Cue, Inc.
Alan Colvin

8. Red Star Fish Bar
Idea 21 Design
Tom Berno, Jeff Davis

9. Abaltat
DETAIL. DESIGN STUDIO

10. Yellow Bike Project Austin
Idea 21 Design
Tom Berno, Jeff Davis

11. Morningside Athletic Club
Cue, Inc.
Alan Colvin

12. Icarus Digital
Organic Grid
Michael McDonald

13. Renaissance Capital
Langton Cherubino Group
Jim Keller, Janet Giampietro, David Langton

14. Mill Valley Film Festival
MINE™
Christopher Simmons, Tim Belonax

15. GO
Fitzgerald+CO/Deep Design
Heath Beeferman, Matt Blackburn, Greg Feist

16. Convergence
MINE™
Christopher Simmons, Tim Belonax

17. ArtServe
Square One Design
Mike Gorman, Lindsay Jones

18. Neustar
Siegel+Gale
Sven Seger, Young Kim, Lloyd Blander, Jong Woo Si, Enshalla Anderson

19. Warehouse 242
Eye Design Studio
Gage Mitchell, Chris Bradle, Steve Whitby

20. Aquarius Advisors
John Langdon Design

21. Radlyn
Cue, Inc.
Alan Colvin

22. Bibo
Ó!
Einar Gylfason

23. Pfizer
Siegel+Gale
Howard Belk, Sven Seger, Young Kim, Johnny Lim, Monica Chai, Quae Luong, David McCanless

24. California Film Institute
MINE™
Christopher Simmons, Tim Belonax

25. Fujiken Setsu
Christopher Dina
Christopher Dina, Yukari Dina, Katsumasa Sekine

26. Vocii
Tandemodus
Kelly Komp, Andy Eltzroth, Charee Klimek, Classic Color, Bill Borque

27. Crush Wine Bar
Idea 21
Tom Berno, Jeff Davis

28. Shop Gopher
Jan Sabach Design

29. LOUD Foundation
Seven25. Design & Typography
Isabelle Swiderski

30. PopTech!
C2
Erik Cox and John Bielenberg

31. Frank at the AGO
Hahn Smith Design
Nigel Smith, Alison Hahn, Richard Marazzi, Fred Tan, Emily Fung

Color choices can't be made entirely objectively, but most of the time (we hope) you'll make color choices for reasons that add up to more than a gut reaction.

CB
1

K
2

3

NEU★ FUND LAND
4

5

6

SEVENDOAKS
7

8

9

10

11

12

13

14

GO
15

C
16

17

neustar™
18

19

20

21

bibo
22

Pfizer
23

cfi
24

K
25

26

CRUSH
27

28

LOUD
29

POP! TECH
30

FRANK
31

5 Applied Color

As color spreads across an identity program into environments, packaging, websites, and more, consistency and meaning reign supreme.

Strong identity programs use color in a fiercely consistent fashion. Choosing the right color is important—if you end up owning the wrong one, you can drag down a brand—but the importance of consistency in application can't be overstated. Anything less adds confusion to the emotional spectrum that inspired the color choice in the first place.

As you think about how a base color and its accents tie a program together, remember this: Color communicates at the speed of light. The brain responds to color the same way it responds to pleasure or pain. It's immediate, primal. Know the cultural connotations of colors before assigning meaning to them within your identity program. Green means "go," but it can also mean environmentally friendly, or the Brazilian national football team.

Some program designers pick one color and stick to it.

1

2

Some designers pick a palette within which to work and make color selections based on the application.

1. Bags
Push
Chris Robb, Mark Unger, Gordon Weller, Forest Young, Randall Morris, Renda Morton, Pedro Gomez, Steven Marshall

2. London Design Festival 2009
Pentagram
Domenic Lippa

3. Kuhlman
Imagehaus
Jay Miller, Mahsa Safavi-Hansen, April Mueller

4. Ila
Pentagram
John Rushworth

3

4

6 Color Power

Clinical and anecdotal tests on color psychology and emotion have led to the development of widely accepted theories about color. That's why schools and hospitals favor teal paint for interior walls to make people feel calm, while restaurants are more likely to choose red interiors to make people feel hungry. But the power of certain colors changes over time and across cultures.

One cannot deny the influence of fashion industry trends on color choices. Seasonality in fashion markets creates programmed obsolescence: What is the new "black" this season? Color-trend experts try to predict what car colors consumers might want to buy in the future. These color trends cross markets freely and often. A popular lime-green highlight on a Prada bag might find its way into business cards, websites, interiors, or office chairs.

Culture also plays a role in how colors are interpreted. The obvious example: In Western cultures, people wear black to funerals, while in Eastern cultures mourners wear white. The cultural connotations of color are often learned and permeate a market.

What can brown do for you? How about pink? Red? Orange? Some organizations work hard to "own" a color and make it a foundational element of their brand.

3 Urban Legends About Color

SOURCE
Leatrice Eiseman
Executive Director, The Pantone Color Institute
colorexpert.com
eisemancolorblog.com

One of the most important things to remember about making informed color choices is to get your information from current sources—not material that was written sixty years ago. Some companies have associated their brands with colors in open defiance of the old urban legends—and have done it so beautifully and elegantly that they have redefined the associations made with those colors.

1. "Orange is a fast-food color"
That was the feeling in the 1950s and '60s, when fast food first appeared and much of the signage that was created for that fledgling industry was connected to the color orange. But if Hermès is using orange, that should tell you that it's not a plastic, fast-food color anymore.

2. "Blue evokes tranquility"
It is unwise to put such a wide umbrella over an entire color family. We all know there are many variations within the blue family. Any blue that is close to a wonderful blue sky might feel tranquil, because people all over the world see the beautiful blue sky and associate it with comfort and play. If, however, the blue starts to approach an electric blue or a blue flame, the color begins to possess some of the same dynamic and attention-getting qualities usually associated with reds.

3. "Use bright colors when designing for Latinos"
There are a lot of cultural generalities made about color—this is just one. It is best to avoid them all. First of all, not everybody living in Rio de Janeiro has a Latino background. And even though the Latino population in every part of the world might embrace their ethnic heritage, they also swim with the broader population. Let the best, most current thinking inform your design, and question stereotypes wherever you encounter them.

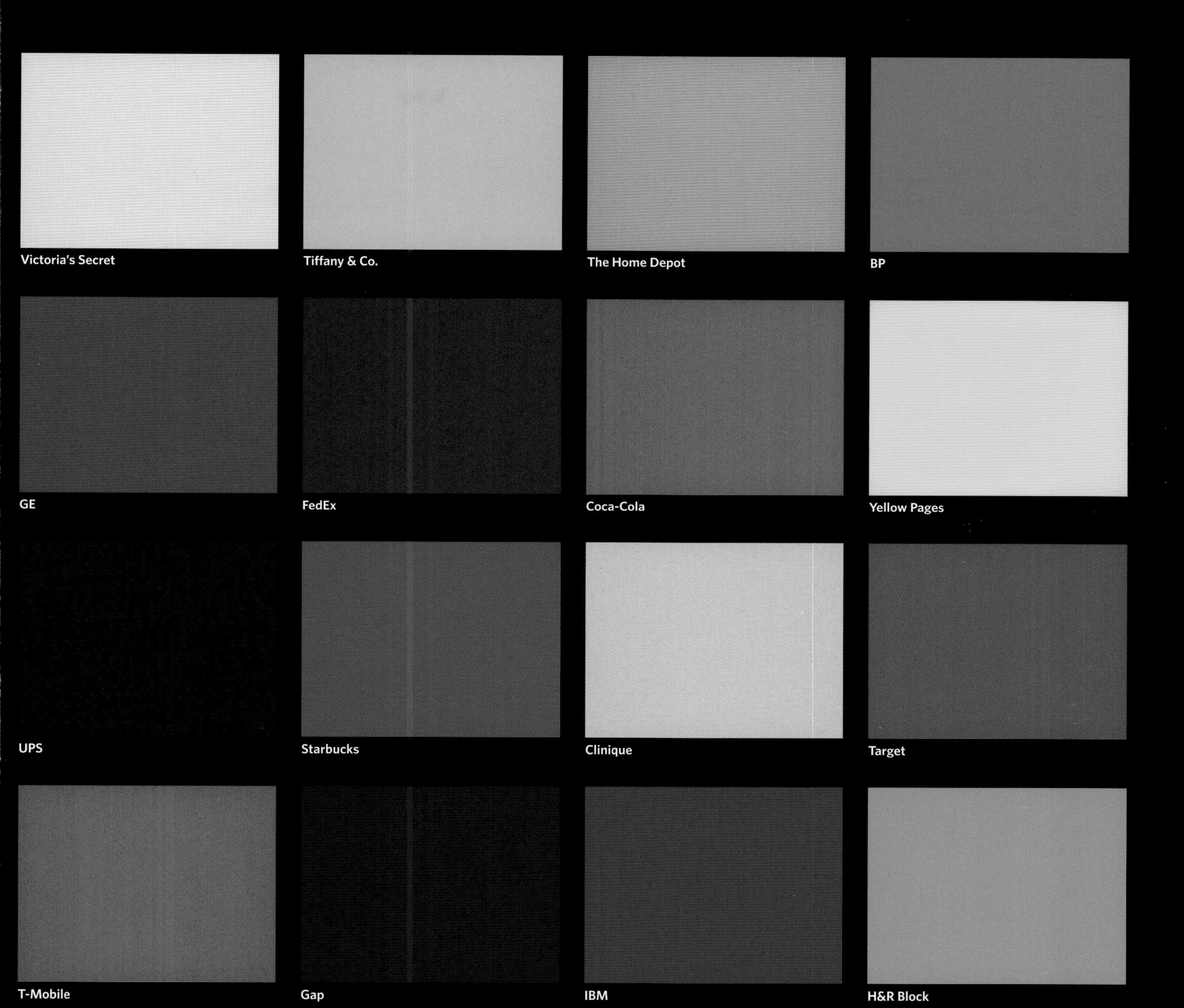
Victoria's Secret
Tiffany & Co.
The Home Depot
BP
GE
FedEx
Coca-Cola
Yellow Pages
UPS
Starbucks
Clinique
Target
T-Mobile
Gap
IBM
H&R Block

7 3-D Logos

Graphic identities typically take two-dimensional form, but many identity programs beg the opportunity for marks to live in three dimensions. When they do, interesting questions and risks emerge.

Should a logo stylized to look spherical actually become a sphere in signage? How should a logo be viewed from the side? Should a logo composed of three horizontal bars be interpreted as three rectangular blocks or three cylinders? Is this open for artistic interpretation, or is there a correct manifestation of the symbol?

When venturing into this territory, a larger issue emerges quickly: whether a logo exists inherently as a symbol of a thing, or—if given the opportunity—as the thing itself. In our view, this answer is clear. A logo is a symbol. Making a logo into a piece of sculpture risks confusing its readability as a symbol. On the other hand, other treatments may add interest.

Two-dimensional application methods such as paint or vinyl don't change the meaning of a mark. Creating readable outdoor signage often involves making raised, cut out, or extruded shapes and letterforms. This can be a reliable technique, provided the substrate thickness enhances, rather than interferes with, the readability of the mark.

1

2

3

4

Environmental graphics sometimes raise the question of whether or not to create a 3-D logo.

5

1. Spectator Group
Studio International
Boris Ljubicic, Igor Ljubicic

2. Gallery C
Evenson Design Group
Stan Evenson, Mark Sojka

3. Schlegel Bicycles
S Design, Inc.
Sarah Sears, Cara Sanders Robb, Jesse Davison

4. The Dorchester Collection
Pentagram
John Rushworth

5. IGH
Studio International
Boris Ljubicic

8 Physical Elements

As identity programs make their way into physical spaces, they present golden opportunities for amplifying brand attributes. Concepts suggested in the two-dimensional mark—translucency, shape, color, contrast, etc.—can be realized in sophisticated, surprising, and enlightened ways when they move into three-dimensional space.

Well-executed programs demonstrate the personality or character of the brand through details of interior and exterior architecture as well as signage. Logos should be treated with care, but pulling other program elements into a physical space is a fantastic way to build a brand beyond the logo. Many other factors, constraints, and opportunities come into play here—including readability, materials, scale, distance, proximity, atmosphere, wayfinding, and experience design.

The Apartment Identity
The Luxury of Protest
Stefan Boublil, Peter Crnokrak

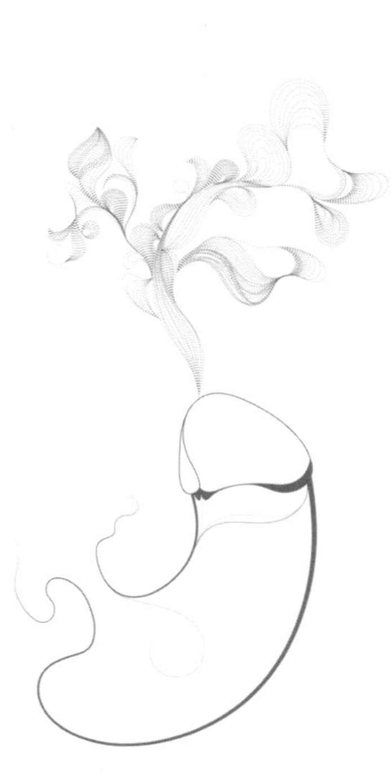

Posts and banners echo the rainbow in the mark for la Gare het Station to create memorable spaces with brand continuity.

La Gare - Het Station
Hoet & Hoet
Ronane Hoet, Carolina Villamizar, Hellen van Mil

9 A Sense of Place

Like colors on an artist's palette, program elements in a physical space mix together to paint a cohesive picture. This introduces an important opportunity for creating a compelling brand experience.

The most successful retail chains and product showrooms excel at creating meaningful, ownable brand identities within their commercial environments. Think about how materials, color, and space come together to deliver different customer experiences at a Starbucks store as opposed to Victoria's Secret or Costco. How big is the front door? What color are the walls? How low is the ceiling? How wide are the aisles? How are the products arranged? Where is the cashier?

When working to translate a brand into a physical environment, look for inspiration in any impactful space that leaves an impression: a five-star hotel, New York City's Central Park, an art museum, a corporate lobby. Good brand identities express a sense of place.

Physical spaces present an opportunity to envelop the customer in a brand experience. Consider the experience you are trying to create and whether the physical environment helps deliver it.

1. Tihany Design
Mirko Ilić Corp
Mirko Ilić

2. Blue Bamboo Yoga
Zync
Marko Zonta, Mike Kasperski, Peter C. Wong

3. The Dorchester Collection
Pentagram
John Rushworth

1
2

10 Contrast in Composition

Contrast makes marks distinguishable. As a rule, the less contrast a mark has—both internally and with its surroundings—the harder it is to make it stand out.

The phrase "graphic identity" implies high contrast. A "graphic" identity has graphic form—it lives as an abstracted, simplified, high-contrast symbol of something. Good graphic identities often use contrast to draw a comparison between two things. Usually that comparison begs a conversation, leading the viewer to wonder: Why is the weight of this letter different than that one? Why is this shape different than all the rest? And what does this all mean? Is it a joke? Does it suggest some deeper meaning? Does it imply variety, evolution, individuality?

Contrast is a powerful tool in designing well-composed, meaningful graphic identities.

1

2

3

4

5

MEETING
PRODUCTIONS
INC. Quality Event Planning

6

The intentional juxtaposition of two elements—weight, color, typeface, orientation, etc.—can enhance meaning or simply add interest.

1. Rod Ralston
circle k studio
Julie Keenan, Jack Anderson

2. UNRESERVED
The O Group
Jason B. Cohen, J. Kenneth Rothermich

3. Garza Architects
Murillo Design, Inc.
Rolando G. Murillo

4. Convince and Convert
Bohnsack Design
Chris Bohnsack

5. Boston Ballet
KORN DESIGN
Denise Korn, Ben Whitla

6. Meeting Productions
Xose Teiga

7. House of Cards
Pentagram
Domenic Lippa

8. Fingerprint Strategies
Spring Advertising
Perry Chua, Rob Schlyecher, James Filbry, Jan Perrier, Chris Coulos

9. Kihoku
Christopher Dina

HOUSE OF CARDS

7

FINGERPRINT

8

KIHOKU

9

11 Contrasting Elements

Contrast is relative to the things around it. If you're looking at a mark on a high-resolution backdrop (a piece of white paper), then it doesn't need to be high contrast to be legible. In fact, if contrast is too high, even a sophisticated mark can look crude.

When applied as part of an identity program, the mark must contrast from its surroundings. This may seem obvious, but it can be a challenge in practice.

In program application, contrast not only deals with graphic elements such as color and scale, but also substrate, ambient light, backlighting, reflection, texture, angle, translucency, movement, time, and interaction—just to name a few. So, if someone says, "Make the logo bigger," your solution could be to make it red, or make everything else gray, or put a tint behind everything else. Making a logo bigger is certainly one way to heighten the contrast between it and its surroundings, but it's only one of many ways to do so.

1

1. Space 47
joe miller's company
Joe Miller

2. NEUFUNDLAND
Simon & Goetz Design GmbH & Co. KG
DörteFischer, Julia Brett, Heiko Winter

3. Bus Stop
gdloft PHL
Allan Espiritu, Matthew Bednarik

2

3

These graphics are designed to stand out by using colors and shapes that contrast with their surroundings.

12 Being Different

Strong brand identities not only stand in contrast with their top competitor(s), but also with the overall market landscape. Contrast in brand identity begins with positioning, which should focus on points of differentiation, and can be reflected through graphic style, program application, and meaning.

Brand identities that use contrast well stand out based on how they look, feel, and behave differently than the rest of the market. For example, a brand identity built on Apollo-era NASA engineers and classic TV cop shows helps Geek Squad stand out among computer tech support companies.

Of course, as competition makes standing out harder, designers must dig deeper. Increasingly, differentiating a brand means looking for blue oceans—new, uncontested markets ripe for growth. When others zig, try zagging.

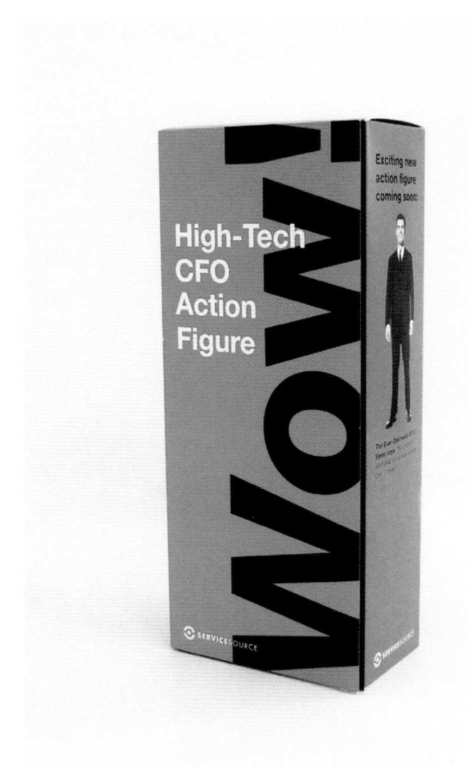

This high-tech CFO action figure helps Service Source stand out in its market.

Service Source
C2
Erik Cox, Greg Galle, John Bielenberg, Marc O'Brien

13 Logo Shapes

An assemblage of different shapes often comprises a graphic identity. At the same time, graphic identities form a single shape once assembled. A logo's internal shapes largely define it, since other aspects such as color may change over time or in different contexts. Which shapes are selected and how their interplay unfolds can become memorable components of a graphic identity: Are they contained or freeform? Complex or simple? Thick or thin? Symmetrical or asymmetrical? Singular or multiple?

Many logos strive for a sense of balance or simplicity by employing a circle or square as its primary external shape. Like word marks that are recognized before they are read, the overall shape of a logo becomes a recognizable identifier for a brand.

What type of company is a circle? A square? A triangle? An egg shape? Shape, like color, makes an immediate impact. What shape will people remember about your graphic identity?

1. Mexipor
Xose Teiga

2. Evenson Design Group (EDG)
Evenson Design Group
Stan Evenson, Mark Sojka, Dallas Duncan, Tim Moraitis

3. Bus Stop
gdloft PHL
Allan Espiritu, Matthew Bednarik

4. Corporation Engtransstroy
fallindesign
Svetlana Faldina, Anastasia Faldina, Alexandra Faldina

5. PopTech!
C2
Erik Cox, John Bielenberg

6. Rooster
TOKY Branding + Design
Eric Thoelke, Jamie Banks-George

7. Campbell Mithun
Cue, Inc.
Nate Hinz, Alan Colvin, Paul Sieka

8. Sandy Leong
The O Group
Jason B. Cohen, J. Kenneth Rothermich

9. Charlie Palmer at the Joule
Mirko Ilić Corp
Mirko Ilić, Jee-eun Lee

4

5

6

7

8

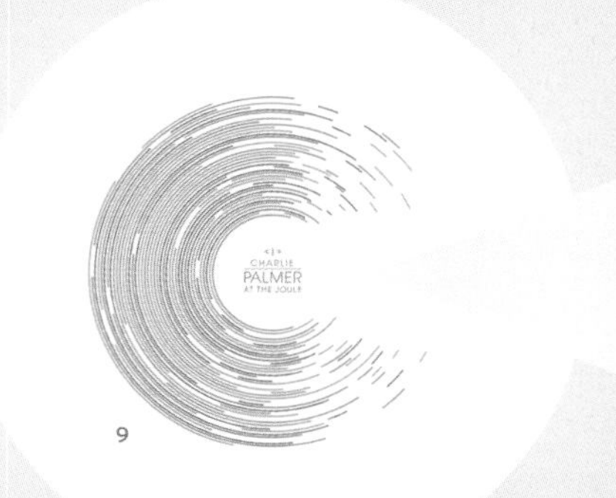

9

14 Shape Patterns

It can be very effective to borrow shapes from a graphic identity to create program elements. Shapes that echo the logo (squares for a square-ish logo, circles for a circular logo, etc.) can be used to create pattern or texture. These elements not only are useful in making the look of the program more cohesive, but they also can help make the graphic identity more meaningful and memorable.

More information is conveyed as program designers translate a graphic identity into physical spaces, allowing for layers of meaning to enrich the identity program. Consistent use of these shape elements will remind the viewer of the logo without being redundant.

Dominant shapes in the logo can create a visual motif for program elements. For La Fonda del Sol, the round sun logo becomes a letter *O* in window signage; for Circo, the red letter *O* becomes a recognizeable graphic element. For Neustar, a simple diagonal creates a recognizable pattern.

1. La Fonda del Sol
Mirko Ilić Corp
Mirko Ilić, Jee-eun Lee

2. Circo by Target
circle k studio
Julie Keenan, Karen North, Nicolas Aparicio, Chris Lehmann

3. Neustar
Siegel+Gale
Sven Seger, Young Kim, Lloyd Blander, Jong Woo Si, Enshalla Anderson

LA FONDA DEL SOL
1

circo
ALL ONE FLAVOR

circo

circo

circo

2

neustar
Collaborate
Solving the world's most complex communications challenges by making networks smarter.
MacBook Air
2009 / ANNUAL REPORT
neustar
neustar
99.999%

neustar™

3

15 Shape and Meaning

Identity programs can reinforce brand identities by echoing or suggesting brand promises. Simple treatments might suggest ease of product use. Patterns might suggest energy associated with customer service. Audiences see big and bold treatments as accessible, while small and understated graphics might suggest exclusivity. Shapes can also be used to illustrate a product or service, either literally or figuratively. Shapes can build on each other to tell a brand story and enhance the meaning of a brand identity.

The Go logo references two primary shapes—a circle and an arrow—to convey a sense of the product in use (a golf ball being driven forward) on packaging and the product itself.

GO
Fitzgerald+CO/Deep Design
Heath Beeferman, Matt Blackburn, Greg Feist

LONG

STRAIGHT

LONG

STRAIGHT

LONG
LONG

STRAIGHT
STRAIGHT

16 Cultural Symbols

We live in a world of complex symbology, where symbols with deep cultural roots are modified, editorialized, and juxtaposed to create ever-new meaning. Graphic designers often serve as interpreters (or reinterpreters) of cultural symbols through graphic identities.

From the flags of nations to religious icons to the classical elements (earth, water, air, fire, and ether) of ancient philosophies, symbols communicate big ideas in small packages. Designers inherently recognize the power of symbols. As the world gets smaller and more interconnected, we need to be increasingly mindful of where that power comes from.

It's impossible to divorce symbols from cultures. That's why the same organization is known as the Red Cross Society in one part of the world, and the Red Crescent Society in another. Launching a brand that spans cultures and relies on symbols requires research and diligence to ensure that the symbols have similar meaning in different parts of the world. Symbols inspired by nature present less risk because they are so universal.

1

2

3

Symbol languages from the worlds of technology, law, gaming, sports, or elsewhere might layer meaning onto a brand by way of a graphic identity that builds upon a symbol from one of these subcultures.

1. Mediterranean Games
STUDIO INTERNATIONAL
Boris Ljubicic

2. Japan-India Friendship Year 2007
Christopher Dina

3. Himneskt
Ó!
Einar Gylfason, Trausti Traustason

4. Omidyar Network
Hot Studio Inc.
Henrik Olsen, Margot Merrill, Han Wang, Eric Grant, Brian van Veen, Holly Hagen, Kathy Simpson

5. Doc Ditto
Meta Newhouse Design
Meta Newhouse, Ben Barry

6. Reloaded
Cacao Design
Mauro Pastore, Masa Magnoni, Alessandro Floridia

7. C Plus
MINE™
Christopher Simmons, Tim Belonax

8. Game Investors
Volume Inc.
Adam Brodsley, Eric Heiman, Marcelo Viana

9. So Single
Cacao Design
Mauro Pastore, Masa Magnoni, Alessandro Floridia

10. Swiss Yachts
LOOVVOOL
Hannes Unt, Valter Kaleta

ON
OMIDYAR
NETWORK™

4

5

6

7

GAMEINVESTORS.COM

8

9

SWISS YACHTS

10

17 Symbol Vocabularies

Many identity programs integrate a system of symbols, drawing on the graphic identity as a foundation or touchstone for a symbol vocabulary. Extending a mark in this way adds to the brand meaning with a specific function. In a corporate literature system or website, one symbol might suggest sales collateral while another suggests training materials. At the 2014 Winter Olympics in Sochi, Russia, this icon might represent ski jumping, that one, snowboarding.

Symbols should be clear, but often they assume a level of user learning. Provided you use them consistently, your symbol vocabulary will become familiar to your audience and immediate recall will increase. In the U.S., drivers don't think twice about the meaning of a white *H* on a blue rectangular sign (hospital) or a black *X* on a yellow circle (railroad crossing). A collection of consistently applied symbols can create a unique, recognizable graphic language for a brand.

1

Once learned, a system of pictograms can make the reading of washing functions or wayfinding systems more efficient.

1, 2. Infectious Exhibition Icons
DETAIL. DESIGN STUDIO

3. KitchenAid Icons
Thesis
Brian Edlefson, Mark Cook, Amy Cross

CHECKPOINT
STIGMATISED
WINOGRADSKY COLUMN
Abundant microbes in this sealed glass environment will multiply and evolve over the course of the exhibition to create a continuously changing living display. Each species of bacteria is adapted to a different layer of the column yet remains interdependent on the other species in the container.
IMMUNE LAB
Extract some of your own DNA and find out about your immunity to certain diseases while contributing to real research by Trinity College immunologists. Following analysis of your sample in the PCR (Polymerase Chain Reaction) machine, researchers will post test results for secure viewing via the web.
CYBERNETIC BACTERIA 2.0
SIMULATION LAB
CONTAGIOUS CREATIVITY
GLASS VIRUSES
Responding to the ubiquitous media images of artificially coloured viruses, these transparent sculptures challenge our received notions and ask whether some scientific images are designed and used to promote fear.
Luke Jerram, UK
KISS CULTURE
Kiss an agar plate to discover the natural flora you carry on your lips and nose. Your plate once incubated will contribute to the growing wall of cultured kisses on display within INFECTIOUS. Warning: this exhibit contains sterilized horse blood.
Maria Phelan, Ireland
HORDE
An immersive audio visual installation representing the workings of the immune system in the style of an epic Irish myth. Horde explores the complexity of the immune response by drawing parallels between a salmonella infection in the gut and a large-scale ancient battle.
David Bickley, Tom Green & Dr. John Mac Sharry, Ireland
UNDER THE MICROPSCOPE
Examine some of the world's most feared pathogens up close and personal in the INFECTIOUS Microscopy Lab. Check out magnified bacteria such as anthrax and E.coli alongside the immune system cells that help to protect us.

2

3

18 Brands as Symbols

The best brands tend to symbolize something in a culture beyond the specific, pragmatic offer. In rare cases, brands themselves have risen to the level of becoming cultural icons.

When people buy bags prominently displaying the logo of a shoe company, get a tattoo of a computer company logo, or write a song about a car company, you know these brands symbolize something beyond shoes, computers, or cars. When a brand authentically connects itself to an idea that resonates with audiences—health, education, community, etc.—the brand symbolizes more than a business value proposition. Brands that are as much about belonging as they are about buying tend to build the greatest value over time.

What inspires some people to stick a company logo on their car bumper or get it tattooed on their arm?

Photo: Terry Johnston

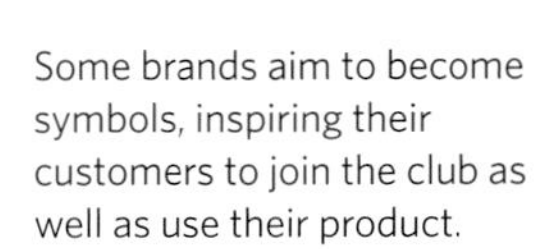

Some brands aim to become symbols, inspiring their customers to join the club as well as use their product.

SWRV
Siegel+Gale
Sven Seger, Doug Sellers, Marcus Barlett, Lloyd Blander

19 Monograms and Word Marks

Monograms and word marks rely on words (typically the initials or name of the organization) rather than pictures to represent an organization graphically, although lots of typographic games blur this line. Context and circumstances should guide decisions about whether or not to use a typographic logo.

When the goal is a mark that's clear and straightforward, type may be best. Of course, that goes out the window if the competitors have all done the same thing. See? Context.

For most organizations, word marks or monograms don't ask the viewer to interpret much. That's not true for organizations with unusual names. The Google word mark challenges customers on a different level than the word mark for Heath Ceramics.

A typographic logo opens up more possibilities than an illustrative symbol. And it's closing fewer doors around the globe for U.S. companies as English has established itself as the language of international business. In a world that's rapidly filling up with symbols (Don't believe it? Check out your computer desktop), a word mark can look very clean, professional, and classic.

1, 2, 3

4, 5

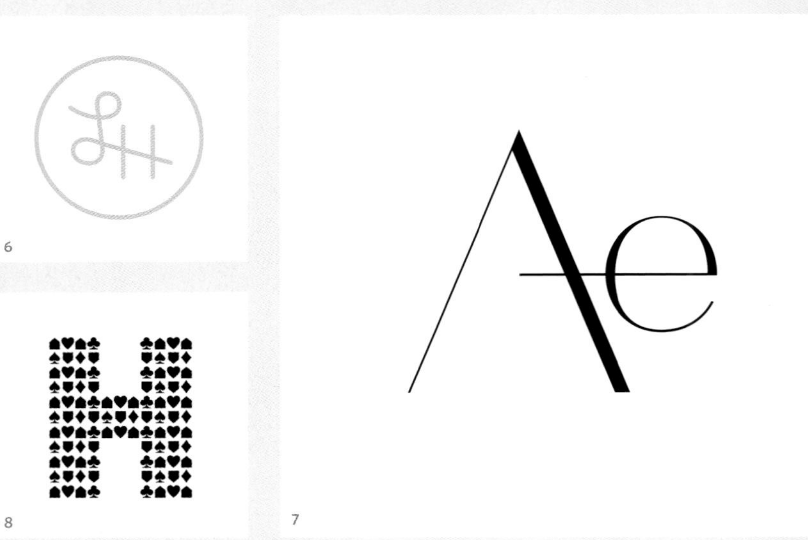
6, 7, 8

Monograms can be inspired by a traditional monogram, varsity letter, or family crest.

1. Caviar Productions
LOOVVOOL
Hannes Unt

2. Niemierko
Bunch
Denis Kovac

3. Fujiken Setsu
Christopher Dina
Christopher Dina, Yukari Dina, Katsumasa Sekine

4. Graceland
Ryan Fitzgibbon

5. altreforme
jekyll & hyde
Marco molteni, Margherita monguzzi, Gaia daverio

6. Live Historic
Partly Sunny
Pat Snavely, Victoria Medgyesi, Daniel Sheehan

7. House of Cards
Pentagram
Domenic Lippa

8. A&E
hopperhewitt
Marcus Hewitt, Susan Hewitt

9. Heath Ceramics
Volume Inc.
Adam Brodsley, Eric Heiman

10. Grand Rapids Art Museum
People Design

11. Romeo
Pentagram
John Rushworth, Sophie Towler, Julian Anderson, Richard Bryant, David Gibbs

12. George at ASDA
Checkland Kindleysides

13. One Fine Art Gallery
50,000feet

14. Humanity
MINE™
Christopher Simmons, Tim Belonax

15. Goodcity
samatamason
Greg Samata, Billie Knipfer

16. Nobli Pasticceria
Cacao Design
Mauro Pastore, Masa Magnoni, Alessandro Floridia, Laura Mangano

9

10

11

12

13

14

15

16

Word marks that employ straight type express the character of a brand in subtle ways.

20 Type Choices

Type has personality. Show us someone who disagrees and we'll show you someone who's the walking embodiment of Times New Roman. Picking the right typeface means picking one that imbues your program with the right feeling. The choice begins with serif vs. sans serif.

The thicks and thins of serif typefaces evolved from the pressure points created by a calligrapher's hand. Given that lineage, serif typefaces often get equated with tradition. By contrast, the relatively younger sans serif typefaces get equated with modernity. However, evidence hints that these personalities are in flux. Sans serif typefaces have been adopted for signage systems all over the world. As a result, what was once seen as quintessentially modern, now can be seen as institutional.

Personality is an important consideration when selecting a typeface, but it should not be the only consideration. Legibility, flexibility, and consistency are also important factors to consider for an identity program.

3

All programs require choices about type. Some programs lead with type when establishing a brand image.

4

FROM THE DESK OF LOLA

alexandra loew
323 571 3531 la
212 655 3045 ny
323 210 7065 fax
alexandra@thedeskoflola.com
6404 hollywood blvd.
suite 205b
los angeles, ca 90028
www.thedeskoflola.com

4

5

1. Proces 15
Bunch

2. Secrecy/Censorship
Anna Filipova

3. Back to Heritage
Bunch
Bunch, Josip Zanki

4. From the Desk of Lola
still room
Jessica Fleischmann

5. The Ellen Theatre
Meta Newhouse Design

21 Type and Meaning

Typefaces may vary, but whenever typography plays an important role in a brand identity, we can assume that the brand is appealing to a reader—someone who appreciates prose, or at least a good headline. They might be a comic book reader as much as a Shakespearean scholar, but, nonetheless, we expect them to read.

As with imagery, typography usually suggests an alternate meaning or cultural context for a brand identity. A typestyle that references classic print ads from the 1950s pushes a brand identity in a very different direction than one inspired by graffiti tags on New York City subway trains from the 1980s.

Typestyles always carry their own history, which often shades the meaning of what is being written. Brand identities built with typographic elements in concert with images may ask a bit more of the viewer than those built with images alone, but they often create deeper and more lasting memories. Some of the most effective campaigns and promotions rely on a headline and an image working together as a single unit. That's why advertising firms continue to partner writers with designers.

cusp

1

Turn Around

2

Sibl ngs.

3

Type can be manipulated to underscore or enhance meaning. For example, the idea of lost siblings is represented by deleting the second *i* in the Siblings word mark.

1. Cusp Conference
samatamason
Dave Mason, Greg Samata, Kevin Krueger, Katie Ingersoll, Christopher Roeleveld, Gena Larsen, Nicholas Paulin, Jason Schifferer, Skot Waldron, Elizabeth Seon, Luis Macias

2. Turanround
Siegel+Gale
Hayley Berlent, Sven Seger, Doug Sellers, Lana Roulhac, Jong Woo Si

3. Siblings
LOWERCASE INC
Tim Bruce, Emilia Klimiuk

4. TypeCon 2009
UnderConsideration
Armin Vit and Bryony Gomez-Palacio

5. Saint Clair
The Creative Method
Tony Ibbotson, Andi Yanto, Mayra Monobe

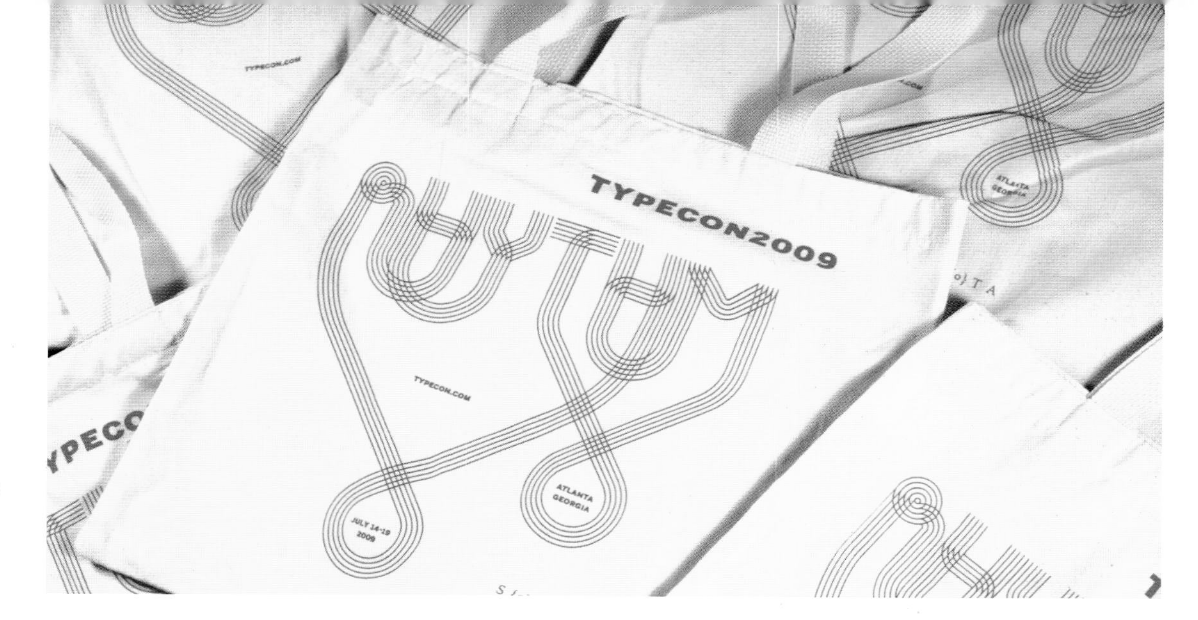

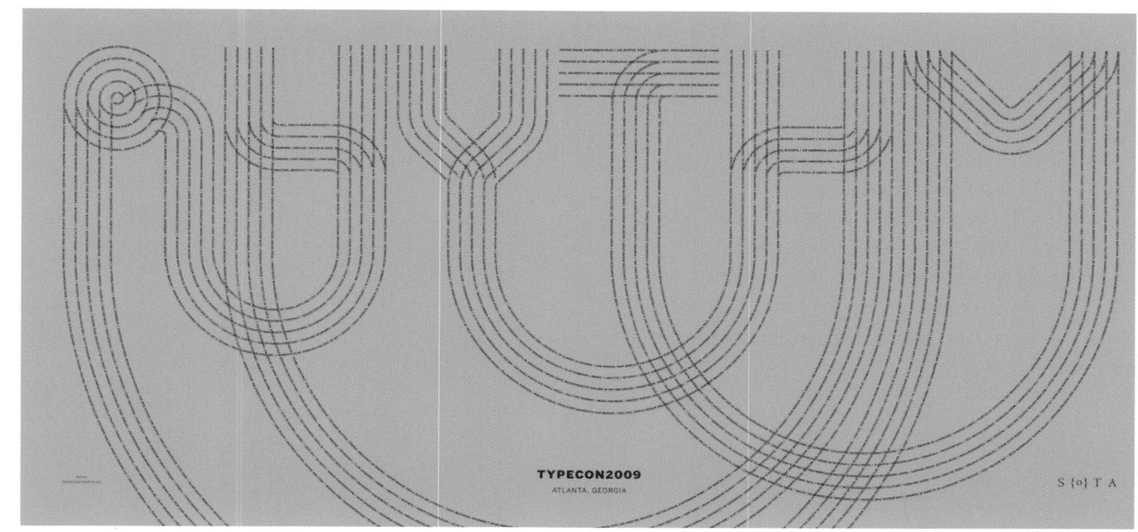

4

5

22 Names and Taglines

An organization's name establishes its most overt identity. Beyond that, a strong name also provides excellent raw material for a strong graphic identity.

An average name won't completely limit the prospects for an organization's graphic identity, but working with a great name can solve half the problem. When paired with a clear graphic device, names that suggest something beyond their literal meanings create some of the most evocative identities. An organization with a great name is an obvious candidate for a word mark. It may make sense to show off the name, keeping any embellishment subordinate rather than layering in meaning with additional graphic elements. A clear, strong name and straightforward type treatment wield surprising power.

Increasingly, organizations are choosing to emphasize separate taglines to help carve out their identity and enhance their positioning. Successful taglines often play off the name, augmenting its meaning. Rebranding initiatives often employ a new tagline when reshaping an organization's identity is the goal but changing the name is not an option.

1

2

3

We don't know what a Workamajig is, but we know there's creativity at work there. Choose a name that will intrigue or inspire.

1. Workamajig
Push
Chris Robb, Mark Unger, Forest Young

2. Cake Monkey Bakery
Special Modern Design
Karen Barranco

3. ASAP
University of Tennessee
Sarah Lowe, Whitney Hayden, Ryan Wodruff

4. Generation Homes
Kevin France Design

5. Elev8
samatamason
David Handschuh, Elizabeth Seon, Greg Samata

6. The Chicken Shack
Idea 21
Tom Berno, Jeff Davis

7. No Frizz by Living Proof
Wolff Olins
Todd Simmons, Tiziana Haug, Sung Kim, Mary Ellen Muckerman, Carmine Montalto, Beth Kovalsky, Michele Miller

8. Relax-a-daisical
Imagehaus
Jay Miller

9. Goodnight Exterminators
Idea 21
Tom Berno, Jeff Davis

4

5

6

~~frizz~~™
Living proof.™

7

8

9

23 Editorial Style

What do product and service names, taglines, headlines, body copy, captions, and sidebars have in common? If you hope to build a successful identity program, let's hope you answered "editorial style." Successful identity programs use a consistent editorial style that addresses their intended audience and remains cognizant of their brand positioning.

Just as a graphic identity sets a visual tone for identity programs, names and taglines set the tone for the program's editorial style. A name that underscores an organization's solid foundation of dependability might lead more naturally into an editorial style that echoes themes of tradition, stability, and trust. On the other hand, an irreverent name or tagline builds an expectation for fun and playfulness in the minds of readers, which should be played out in the editorial style.

Details strengthen identity programs, but programs too often fail to define and pursue an appropriate editorial style across all program literature. If a company could swap out it's competitor's website copy for it's own without the audience noticing the change, that company has missed an opportunity to differentiate itself.

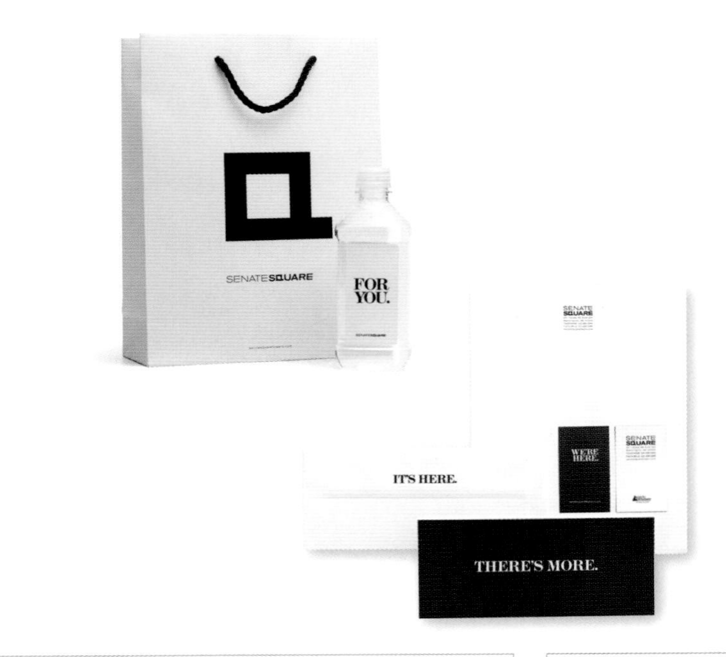

1

1. Senate Square
The O Group
Jason B. Cohen, J. Kenneth Rothermich, Miriam Weiskind, Tal Gendelman, Alex Ammar, Jeff Wolfram, Moment Factory

2. Bretenic Limited
Zync
Marko Zonta, Mike Kasperski

You don't normally want to read an invoice, but here, you'll be glad you did. A conversational editorial style is one way of being engaging and memorable.

2

24 Voice

An organization's name, tagline, and editorial style add up to an important reflection of its brand identity—its voice. As these elements are being developed, consider how the words would sound in the mouth of a brand spokesperson. It's an easy way to personalize the brand voice, and whether or not they use a spokesperson, successful brands have an acute awareness of their voice.

As with all other aspects of brand positioning, when developing a brand voice, look for a different path than the one followed by the competition. If the voice of a company's top competitor sounds slick and technologically savvy, that company might want to consider adopting a friendlier, more approachable voice.

From billboards to bags, brochures to bottles, The Co-operative has a clear voice that speaks directly to its customers.

The Co-operative
Pentagram
Harry Pearce

The **co-operative**

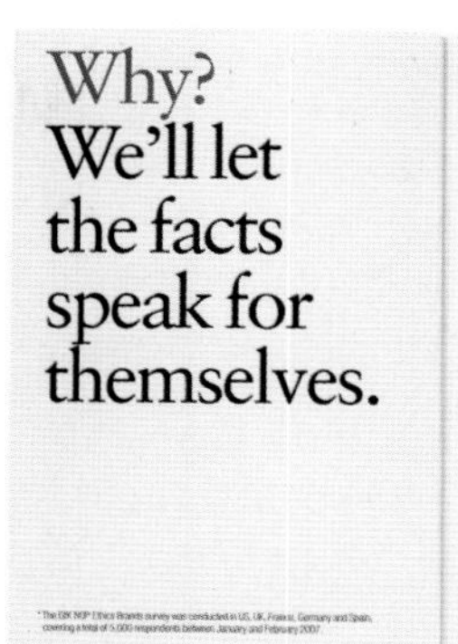

25 Logos as Storytellers

Some logos tell a story. Illustrative marks can depict an object or suggest a scene, either of which can become a powerful brand symbol. A lonely beach chair can hint at a backstory that lends depth to the brand and creates a personal connection with the viewer. Like the cover of a novel, such marks reveal the essence of the story contained therein. The logo is only the beginning of the story, and just like a good book jacket, good logos communicate the story without giving away the ending.

Some logos invite you to write your own ending.

1

Imagine yourself on a beach ...

2

It was night by the water with a glass of wine ...

3

Prepare to enter the Matrix ...

1. The Beach
Gensler
John Bricker

2. Vino Noir
Organic Grid
Michael McDonald

3. Pulse
Siegel+Gale
Sven Seger, Matthias Mencke,
Marcus Barlett, Valerie Fredenburgh

26 Narrative Applications

Programs are all about context, and each place the identity is expressed reveals an opportunity to extend a narrative.

If a graphic identity is the cover of a novel, program elements are the chapters. The first experience with an identity program provides the exposition. As an audience experiences an identity program, consider the sequence, length, and character of each beat in the story.

Consider the where and how of use. Is a sign near the bathroom an opportunity for humor, a reminder of basic hygiene, or both? Is a website intended to surprise or comfort? If there's a television in a lobby broadcasting the news, which channel is it on?

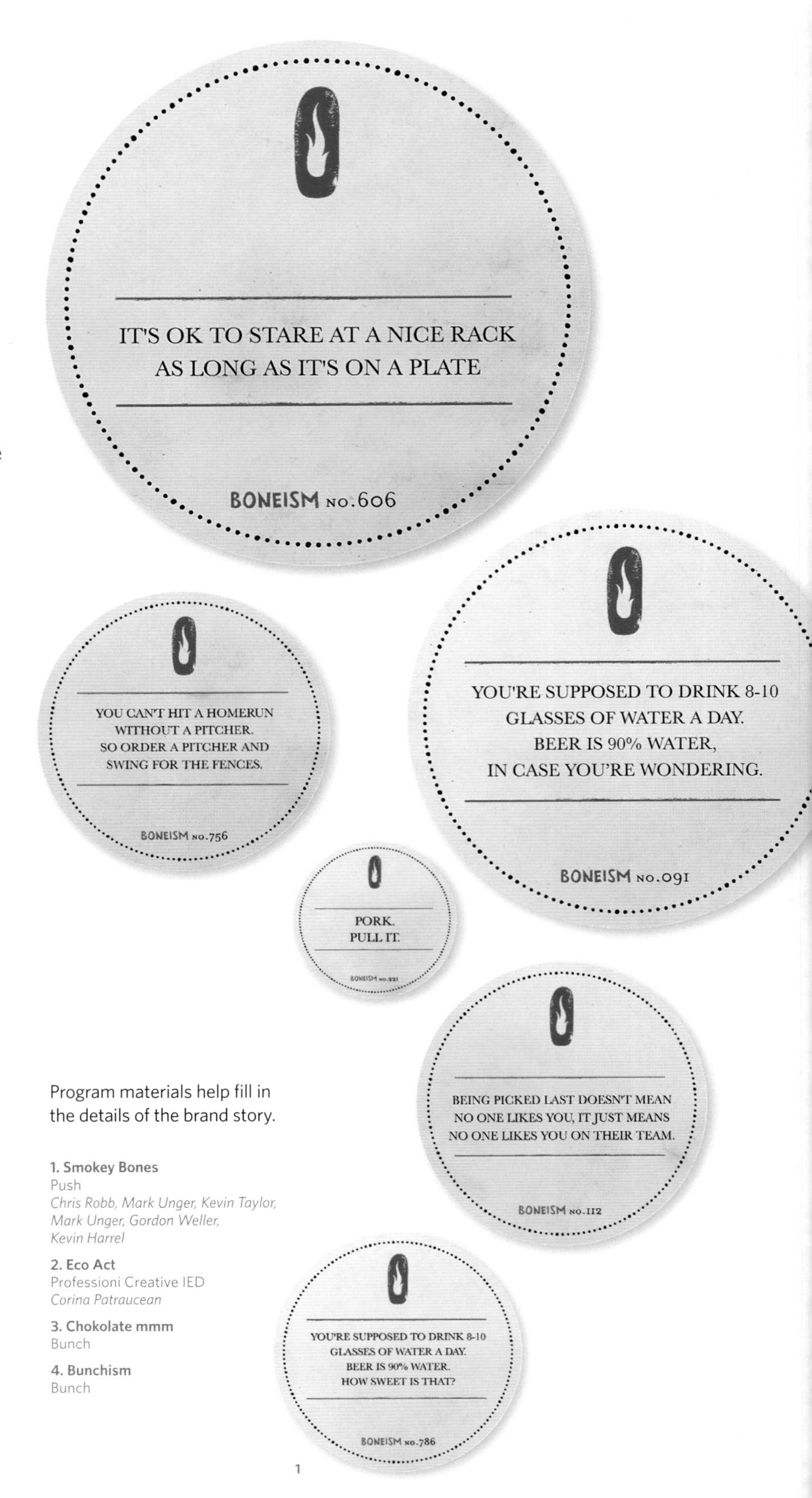

Program materials help fill in the details of the brand story.

1. Smokey Bones
Push
Chris Robb, Mark Unger, Kevin Taylor, Mark Unger, Gordon Weller, Kevin Harrel

2. Eco Act
Professioni Creative IED
Corina Patraucean

3. Chokolate mmm
Bunch

4. Bunchism
Bunch

the most
green gadget
is the one
that you
already own.
act
eco

eco

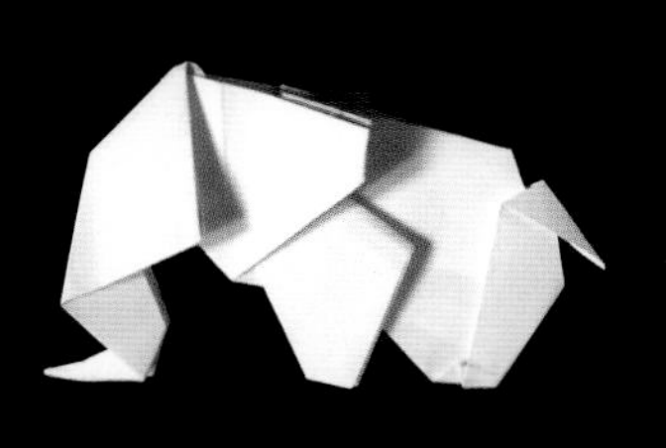

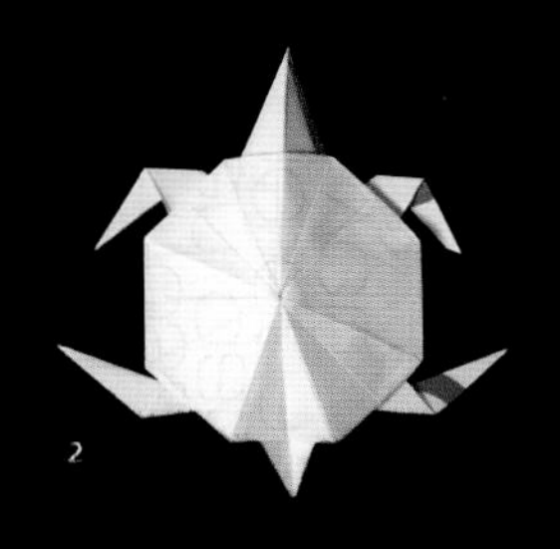

2

Chokolate
Caroline Khouri
Director
Lunch

Chokolate
Caroline Kh
Director

mmm

DAVIS FOR BUNCH

Chokolate

Standard American
Made in Bunch

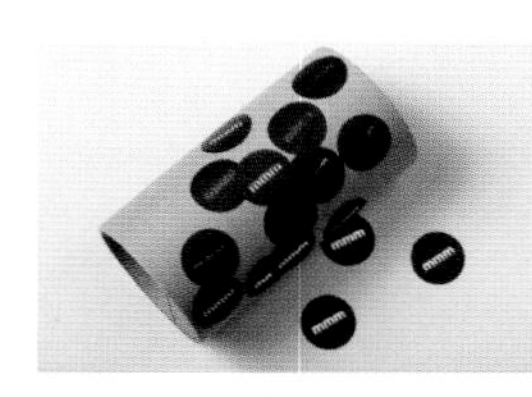

Chokolate
Caroline Khouri
Director

4

Chokolate
With Compliments

With Compliments
Chokolate
With Compliments
Chokolate
With Compliments
Chokolate
With Compliments

3

27 Brand Stories

From religious parables to folk songs to business case studies, stories serve as a primary vehicle for communicating complex ideas in a clear, easily digestible way.

Modern-day brands are promises, and every promise naturally sets a plot in motion: Will the promise be kept or broken? It goes without saying that a brand should keep its promises. They serve as the moral of the brand story—why the "story" was written and what it means to the reader/customer.

Companies with memorable brands not only craft stories that are worth telling, they also live out the morals of their brand stories every day. In today's transparent world, companies are beginning to embrace technology to allow customers and employees to help shape their stories.

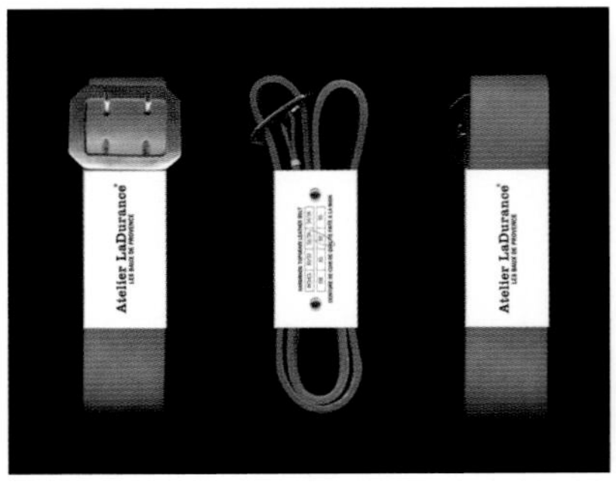

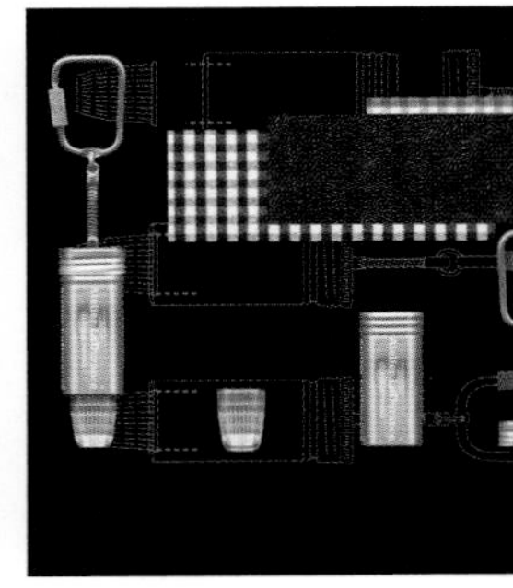

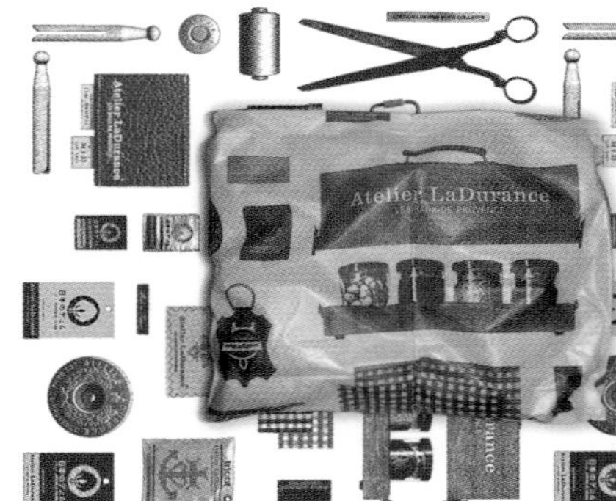

Atelier LaDurance
StormHand
Boy Bastiaens

Atelier LaDurance and Art the Vote invite the audience to play a role in their brand stories.

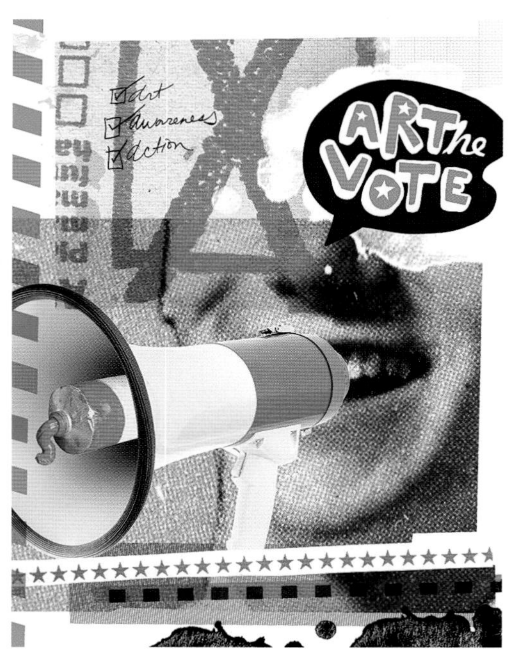

Art the Vote
TOKY Branding + Design
Eric Thoelke, Travis Brown

28 Logo Structure

Structure lays the foundation for being memorable. Nearly every strong mark you'll encounter adheres to an internal structure, a graphic motif. Memorable marks often play games with symmetry or pattern—either it's all about circles or it's all about squares; it's all about what's happening on the top, or it's all about what's happening on the bottom.

Structure brings restraint, order, rhythm, and comfort to a mark. Put care, time, and effort into the exactness of your drawing. There is beauty in the perfection of craft. It also establishes your playing field, making variation more noticeable.

Only once you lay a foundation can you add an effective highlight. Once a designer establishes a base, every move away from that base calls attention to itself.

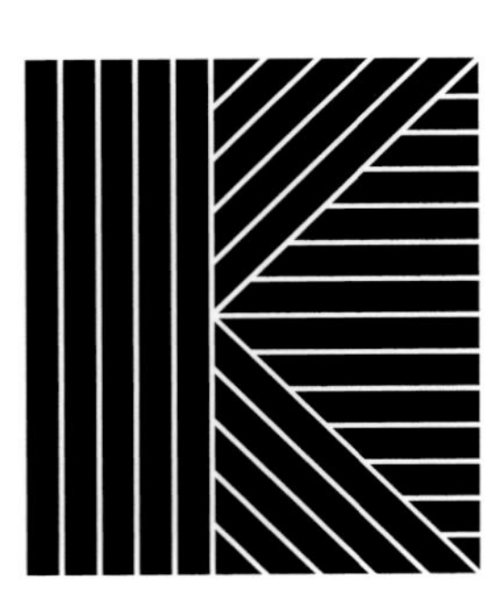

1

2

3

Notice how these marks establish their own rules, and then follow them.

1. Kanuhura
Pentagram
John Rushworth

2. Year
MINE™
Christopher Simmons, Tim Belonax

3. Mill Valley Film Festival
MINE™
Christopher Simmons, Tim Belonax

4. Nahlosa
Diseño Dos Asociados
Víctor Martínez, Juan Carlos García, Carlos Rivera

5. ITP International
MINE™
Christopher Simmons, Tim Belonax

6. Space 47
joe miller's company
Joe Miller

7. Titan
Graphic Communication Concepts
Sudarshan Dheer

8. Vision Spring
UnderConsideration LLC
Armin Vit and Bryony Gomez-Palacio

9. Strategic Hotels
samatamason
Gina Larsen, Greg Samata

4

5

6

7

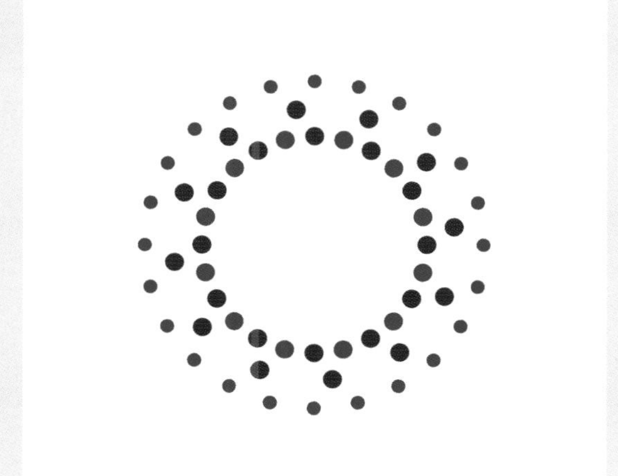

8

9

29 Program Consistency

Maintaining consistency is quite possibly the most difficult aspect of an identity program. But just as internal structure is important to the logo, so too is consistency of application crucial to the program.

If the same structured logo is applied haphazardly, it will be less identifiable. Nothing erodes design value like producing programs—packaging, merchandise, signage, environments, websites, etc.—without consideration to application consistency.

The goal of rolling out a new mark is to strengthen an organization's identity, to make it more recognizable. To achieve this, the identity should be represented in a consistent way across all media and under different constraints—and resist temptations to vary it.

Consistency and exactness are not necessarily synonymous. Notice how product packaging for Smokehouse Market and Daub & Bauble family together consistently while still feeling fresh.

1. Smokehouse Market
TOKY Branding + Design
Eric Thoelke, Jamie Banks-George

2. Daub & Bauble
Wink
Richard Boynton, Scott Thares

1

Daub&Bauble®
MISSION FIG AND THYME
Hand Lotion with Shea Butter
10 fl. oz. (300 ml)
Daub&Bauble®
SORRENTO LEMON AND GINGER
Hand Lotion with Shea Butter
10 fl. oz. (300 ml)
Daub&Bauble®
TAROCCO ORANGE AND CLOVE
Hand Lotion with Shea Butter
10 fl. oz. (300 ml)

2

30 What Is "On Brand"?

Brands are promises, and keeping promises is all about being consistent. In many cases, the promise of a brand stems from the values of an organization's founders. The idea of keeping the brand promise needs to become institutionalized and socialized throughout the organization. But not only do the members of an organization need to understand the brand promise, essentially so do its customers.

People who have no problem identifying a person when he or she is acting out of character often struggle to describe what is in character for the same person. Likewise, identifying brand inconsistency usually comes more easily than recognizing brand consistency. That's why corporate missteps create such public relations nightmares.

Successful brands build a personality with consistent behavior. Decisions about what is appropriate—that is to say, "in character" or "on brand"—for advertising, promotions, products, websites, selling environments, etc., all have the power to build up or erode brand identity.

CASS ART LONDON

The Cass Art brand expression is diverse but easily identifiable.

Cass Art
Pentagram
Angus Hyland

COLEBROOKE ROW
CASS ART LONDON
BRUSHES | PAPERS | CRAFTS
PADS | PAINTS | PORTFOLIOS
DRAWING MATERIALS | GIFTS
CANVASES | EASELS
100'S OF HALF PRICE ITEMS IN STORE
OPEN FOR ART
Stand on the right

OPEN FOR
ART

OPEN FOR
ART
CASS ART LONDON
£5 OFF

CASS ART LONDON
DALER-ROWNEY
system3
ACRYLIC
CASS ART
MANIFESTO
LET'S FILL THIS TOWN WITH ARTISTS
ART IS FREEDOM CASS ART BELIEVES IN ART. WE KNOW THE FREEDOM AND CREATIVE PLEASURE IT BRINGS. SO WE WANT EVERYONE TO REALISE THEY CAN DO IT – AND AFFORD IT.
BEST MATERIALS ARTISTS NEED THE CHOICE OF ALL THE BEST MATERIALS. WE STOCK THE TOP BRANDS FROM AROUND THE WORLD.
BEST PRICES WE NEGOTIATE DIRECTLY WITH ALL THE FAMOUS SUPPLIERS. THEY HELP US, SO WE CAN HELP YOU. THAT'S WHY OUR PRICES ARE AS LOW AS THEY CAN GO.
OUR SHOPS THE SPACE IS DESIGNED TO HELP YOU AND INSPIRE YOU. MATERIALS ARE ORGANISED AND DISPLAYED JUST THE WAY YOU WANT THEM. THE EFFECT IS THOUGHTFUL AND CONTEMPORARY.
OUR PEOPLE OUR STAFF ARE ARTISTS. THEY KNOW ART. THEY ENJOY WORKING WITH WHAT THEY KNOW. THEY GIVE YOU INTELLIGENT AND THOUGHTFUL ADVICE – NO BLUFFING, NO HIDDEN AGENDA.
OUR TOWN WE WANT TO FILL THIS TOWN WITH ARTISTS. WE KNOW LONDON – WE HAVE BEEN HERE FOR OVER 25 YEARS. WE ARE ALSO INDEPENDENT AND CAN GIVE LONDONERS WHAT THEY WANT AND NEED.
CASS ART, BEST CHOICE, TOP BRANDS, LOW PRICES

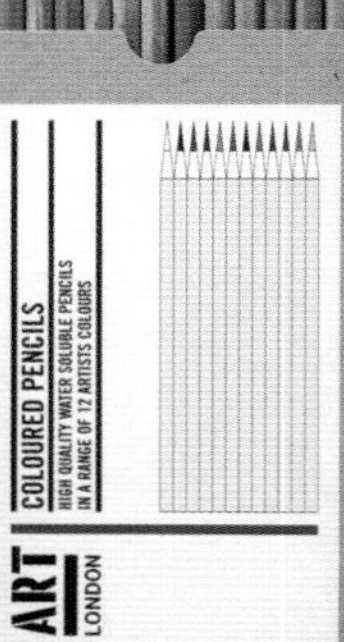
COLOURED PENCILS
HIGH QUALITY WATER SOLUBLE PENCILS
IN A RANGE OF 12 ARTISTS COLOURS
ART LONDON
CASS

Order

31 Logo Flexibility

Inspired by the clever use of variation by media companies such as the music video network MTV, more and more organizations want to change things up with their graphic identities. Logos can be flexible as long as the message is consistent—and consistently recognizable to its intended audience.

Information drives the built-in flexibility within the Language Institute of Central Oregon mark, which uses different colors and icons to signify the organization's different divisions. With the Ringling College of Art and Design, on the other hand, the variations provide little more than decorative interest. In both cases, the ability to change things up provides one of the more distinguishing characteristics of the marks. If more signals were used to vary these marks, however, would you know where to look?

A wide spectrum of attributes spans the chasm between boredom and chaos. In one direction is restraint, structure, rhythm, pattern, and comfort; in the other, highlights, cleverness, creativity, surprise, and capriciousness. Somewhere in the middle is where you might find "good design." Don't underestimate the risks at either extreme.

Ringling College
of Art + Design

1

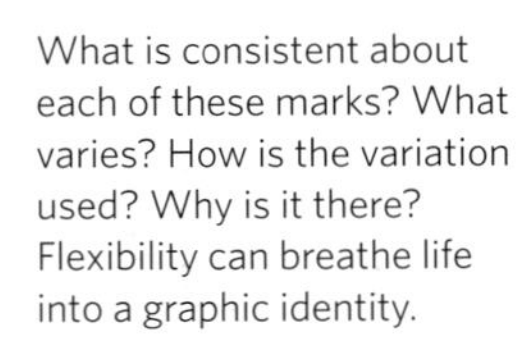

What is consistent about each of these marks? What varies? How is the variation used? Why is it there? Flexibility can breathe life into a graphic identity.

1. Ringling College of Art and Design
samatamason
Kevin Krueger, Dave Mason, Chris Roeleveld

2. Kapulica Studio
Bunch

3. Language Institute of Central Oregon
Sublime Creative Agency
Aileen Walker, William Hastings

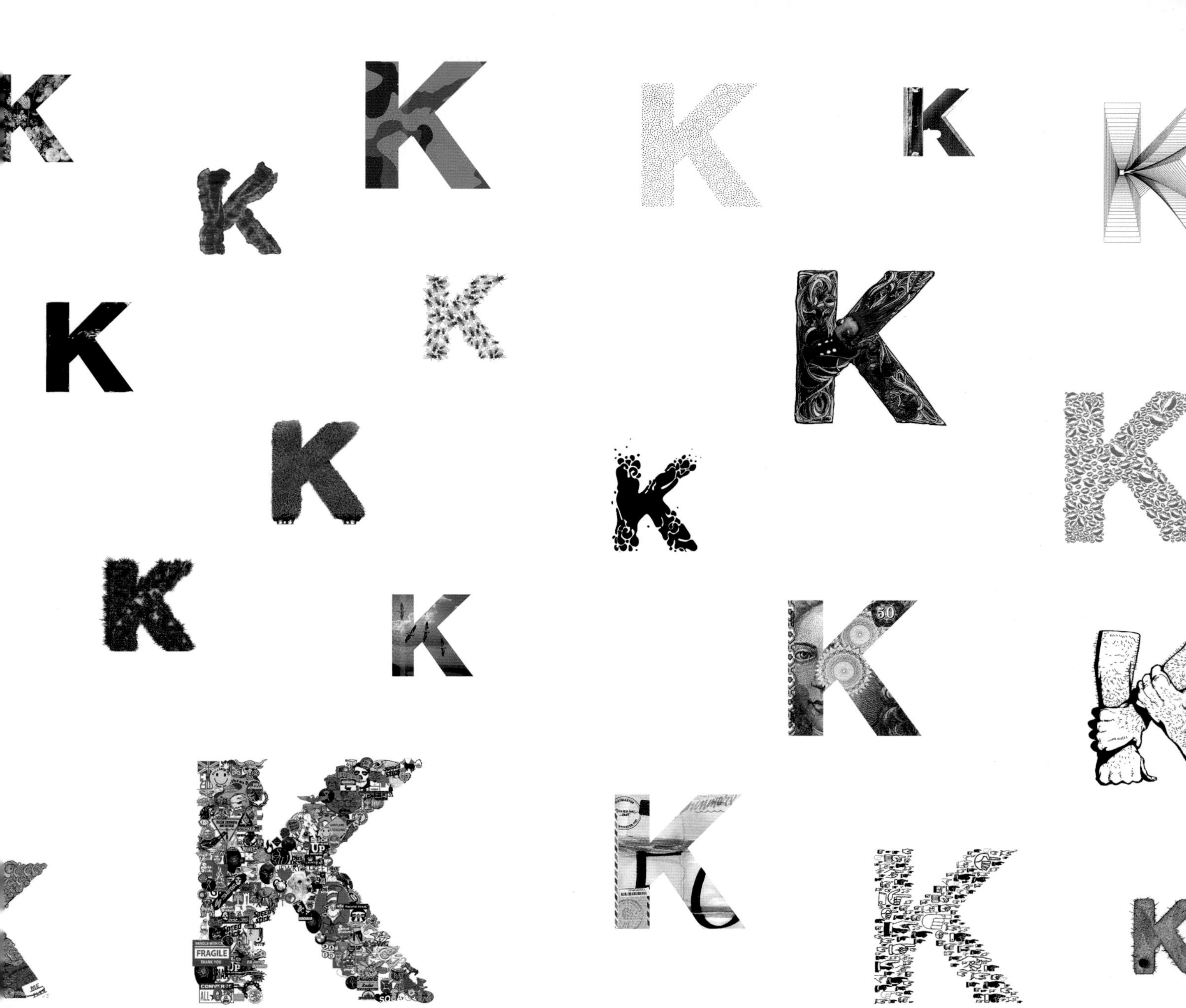

2

language
institute

picaflor
spanish immersion preschool

papillon
french immersion preschool

ni hao
chinese immersion preschool

sakura
japanese immersion preschool

3

32 Flexible Systems

Effective identity programs require enough consistency to be identifiable, but enough variation to keep things fresh and human.

Programs should be designed to not only accommodate variation, but also to carefully orchestrate where variations take place. Whether they highlight certain features or information, variations are an integral part of the program, not an anomaly outside of it. Too often organizations scrap identity programs because they don't include enough built-in variation.

On the other hand, identity programs that accommodate too much variation create their own problems. If you highlight every line of every page in a book, you haven't actually created a single highlight. In fact, if you skipped highlighting one line of one page, that would be a highlight.

Consistency will always set the standard, but the variations of any program typically will become its standout features.

Some programs strive to support system-wide flexibility while holding together as a cohesive whole. The Institut Parfumeur Flores program maintains a generally clean, modern aesthetic while offering a variety of variations on the visual theme of flowers.

Institut Parfumeur Flores
Bunch

PARFUMEUR FLORES

INSTITUT
PARFUMEUR
FLORES

INSTITUT
PARFUMEUR
FLORES

INSTITUT PARFUMEUR FLORES

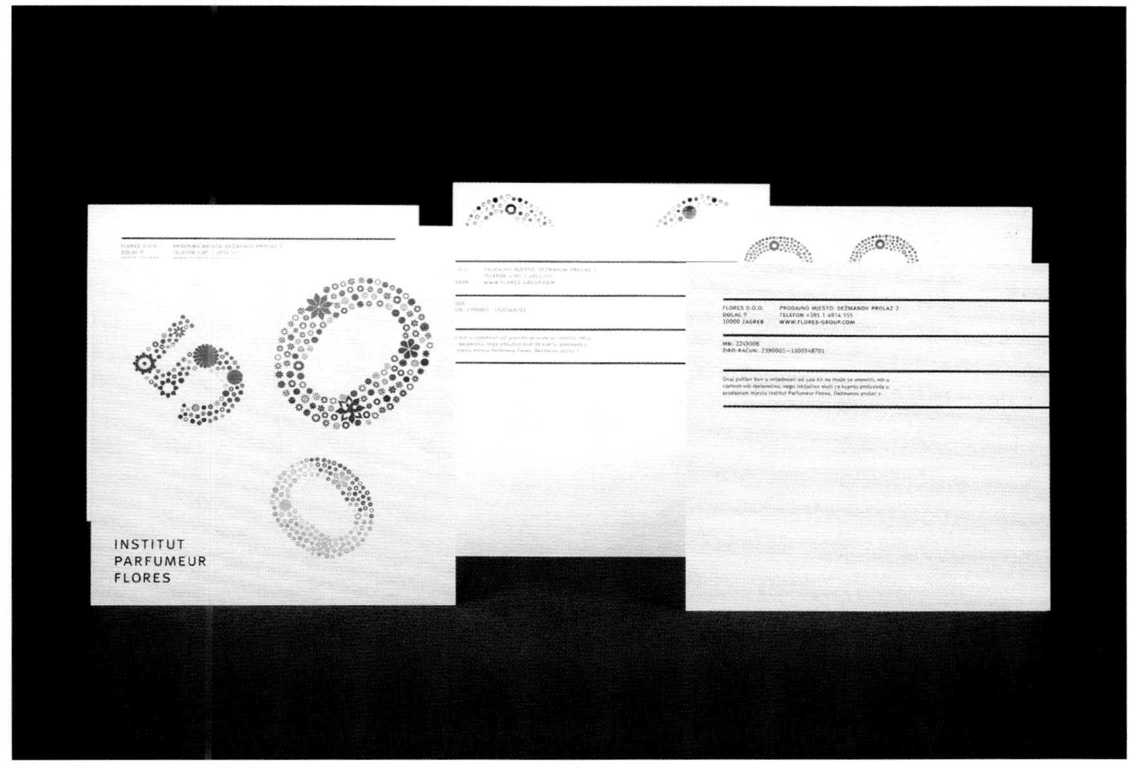
INSTITUT
PARFUMEUR
FLORES

INSTITUT
PARFUMEUR
FLORES

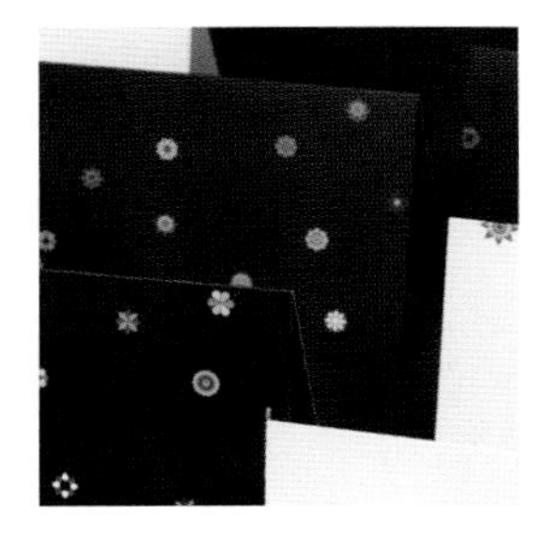

33 Brands that Surprise

Some people don't like surprises. Others can't get enough. Similarly, surprise plays a major role in some brand identities, while others do not tolerate much of it.

You may not wish to find a surprise on your bank statement, but you'd be disappointed if you didn't find a few in a fashion magazine. No customers want things to be boring, which is where absolute consistency with no variation can lead. People like pattern, routine, clubs, affinity groups, etc., but in the words of Aphra Behn, "Variety is the soul of pleasure."

Consider what role surprise can play in any brand identity you help build.

[CURZON • CINEMAS]

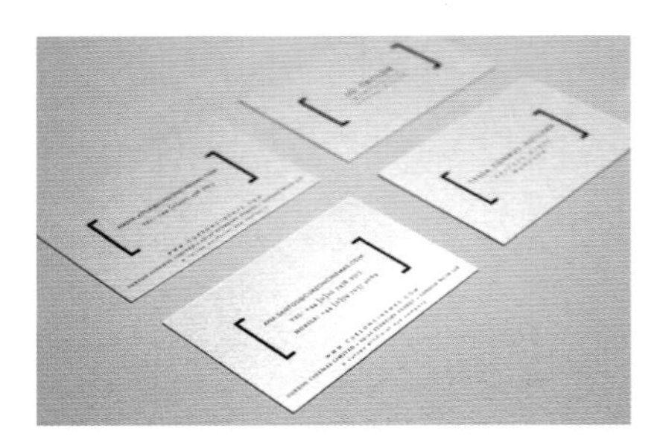

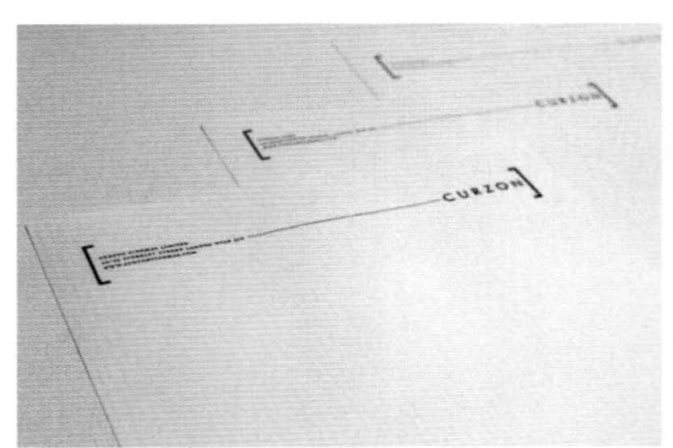

The brand identity developed for Curzon Cinemas stakes a claim on a common graphic element—brackets—but varies their use through clever, lighthearted applications throughout the program, including signage, coupons, and other amenities. Even without the brackets, the identity is strong enough to be easily identified.

Curzon Cinemas
Subtitle.
Michael Salu

CURZON
MAYFAIR
CURZON
Soho
CURZON
RENOIR
CURZON
Chelsea
CURZON
richmond

CURZON
PODCAST

[C]

LIFT

SNACKS

CURZON
MEMBERSHIP
TWO FREE TICKETS
ASK STAFF ABOUT BECOMING A CURZON MEMBER

CINEMAS
KIOSK
TOILETS
WI-FI

BAR

SCREEN
[2]

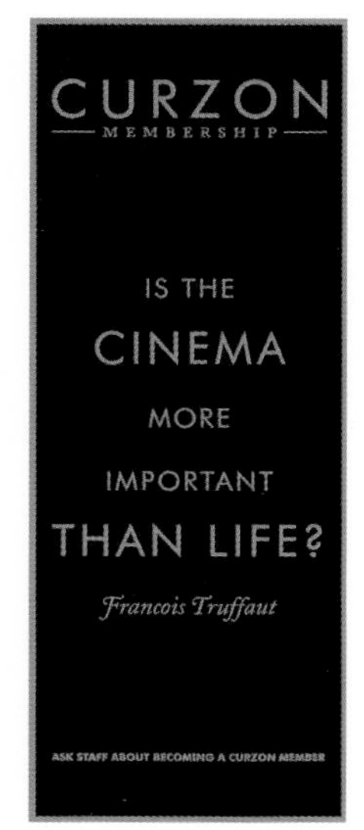

CURZON
MEMBERSHIP
IS THE CINEMA MORE IMPORTANT THAN LIFE?
Francois Truffaut
ASK STAFF ABOUT BECOMING A CURZON MEMBER

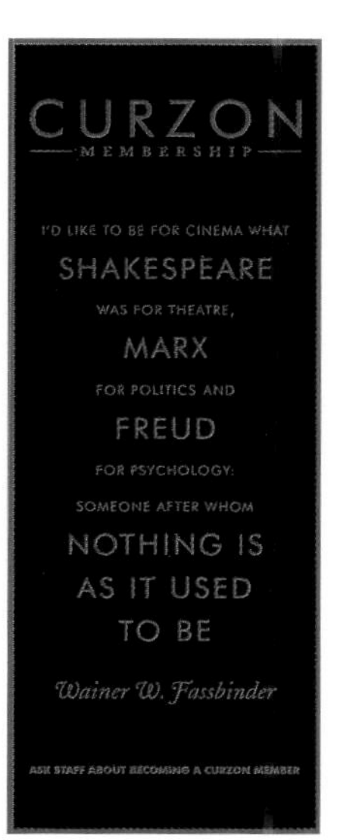

CURZON
MEMBERSHIP
I'D LIKE TO BE FOR CINEMA WHAT SHAKESPEARE WAS FOR THEATRE, MARX FOR POLITICS AND FREUD FOR PSYCHOLOGY: SOMEONE AFTER WHOM NOTHING IS AS IT USED TO BE
Wainer W. Fassbinder
ASK STAFF ABOUT BECOMING A CURZON MEMBER

CURZON
MEMBERSHIP
THE SAVING GRACE OF THE CINEMA IS THAT WITH PATIENCE, AND A LITTLE LOVE, WE MAY ARRIVE AT THAT WONDERFULLY COMPLEX CREATURE WHICH IS CALLED MAN
Jean Renoir
ASK STAFF ABOUT BECOMING A CURZON MEMBER

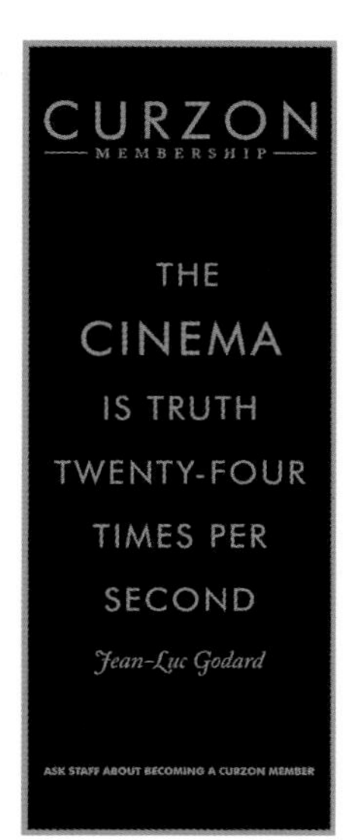

CURZON
MEMBERSHIP
THE CINEMA IS TRUTH TWENTY-FOUR TIMES PER SECOND
Jean-Luc Godard
ASK STAFF ABOUT BECOMING A CURZON MEMBER

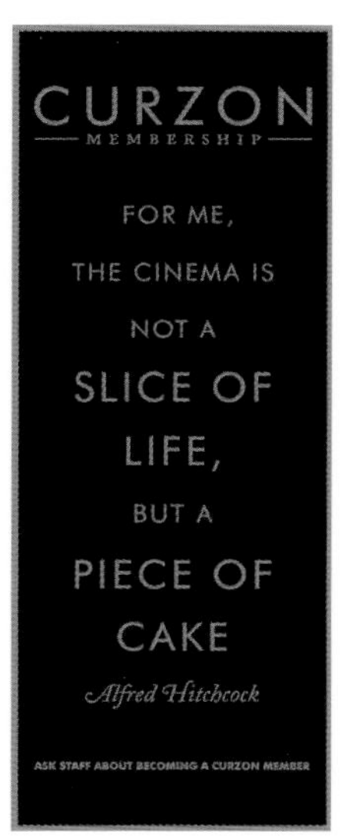

CURZON
MEMBERSHIP
FOR ME, THE CINEMA IS NOT A SLICE OF LIFE, BUT A PIECE OF CAKE
Alfred Hitchcock
ASK STAFF ABOUT BECOMING A CURZON MEMBER

34 Personal Logos

The development of formal graphic identities for companies emerged at about the same time as midcentury modernism. The trend marked a shift from an ad hoc approach to branding to a more deliberate one. Monolithic consistency was the prevailing wisdom, governing how the great captains of twentieth-century industry created recognizable and memorable identities. Today, a new trend has emerged.

Some of the strongest graphic identities of the late twentieth and early twenty-first centuries have challenged this wisdom, gaining notoriety in the process. Cable television vanguard MTV famously versioned its logo based on context (a different treatment for a program like "Yo MTV Raps" vs. "120 Minutes") or whim. Given the fifty-year history of conformity preceding it, this kind of built-in customization suggested the irreverent brand attributes a youth-oriented network desired.

The MTV logo signaled a coming macro trend. In an era of technology-enabled mass customization, consumers increasingly expect to put their own fingerprint on the things they buy and the brands they desire. From manufacturing to information technology to health and wellness, personalization has become the new paradigm. Designers will need to weigh what role customization plays in graphic identity work going forward.

Technology has enabled the audience to express their support for the campaign (or the brand), building an expectation for personalization into some graphic identity design.

Source: "Obamicon.Me" at pastemagazine.com

SARAH
AHABMAN
HOPE
GO BEARS
RELAX MO'
YANG
OBAMICON.ME
"TRAD" MEDIA
THINK
AMBITION
YES I CAN
GOLDILOCKS
FROGRESS
IMPERMANENCE
HOPE
HOPE
CHEESE
THINK !
PEACE
RHYTHM
THINK
HOPE
SHAMWOW
HOPE
BOB
HOPE
HOPE
NOT LUPUS
ARICEBOWL
SMILE :)

35 Inclusive Programs

Good identity programs provide for variation from the start, but the larger trend of customer or user personalization has tested the traditional boundaries of consistency.

An expectation of variety has combined with the ready availability of desktop and online publishing tools to shift emphasis away from the hard rules of conformity one might have found in an identity standards manual a few years ago. In this landscape, the rules loosen as customization and personalization become possible in identity programs. The sort of litmus test for appropriateness you might find in a brand bible might provide all the order a program needs.

Customization and personalization are powerful tools, but they can erode brand recall if used haphazardly. Identity program designers are increasingly challenged to define new kinds of rules for use as well as application. In an increasingly noisy and competitive landscape, successful identity programs will need to draw some lines that should not be crossed.

The audience isn't just listening. They're also making your program their own through customized amenities, and in doing so, they're taking a personal stake in the brand.

1

2

1. Smokey Bones
Push
Chris Robb, Mark Unger, Kevin Taylor, Gordon Weller, Kevin Harrel

2. Bunchism
Bunch

3. Johnson & Johnson Summit
BIG/Ogilvy
Brian Collins, Kapono Chung, Tracy Jenkins, Tadd Kimball, Emily Lessard, Noah Venezia, Charles Watlington

"WHAT
HAPPENS
NEXT?"

Never did
anything Great
all by myself!

I was a nuclear
weapons expert.
Now I meditate.

I HAVE A
HOME IN A
THIRD WORLD
COUNTRY.*

3

36 My Brand

As personalization moves from luxury to expectation, it will no longer serve as a brand differentiator. Leaders in the brand identity space will need to consider the role personalization plays.

It's not likely that all aspects of a customer experience will need to enable personalization. Careful consideration of the customer needs and the brand promise will help define the hallmarks of the brand identity. Whether personalization plays a prominent or secondary role is a strategic choice made by brand managers. As with identity programs, an understanding of the brand identity foundation will help determine how design can best help express a value proposition.

One thing is certain: Consumers like personalization and they're not giving it back. One-size-fits-all solutions will no longer hold up for brands looking to take the lead in their respective industries.

Whether or not brand identities should meet the growing expectation for greater personalization remains a matter of customer need and brand appropriateness.

1. Jones Soda
samatamason
Pamela Lee, Dave Mason, Victor John Penner

2. On Point
Maycreate
Brian May, Monty Wyne, Chris Enter, Nick Turner

3. Chapter Eight
10 Associates
Jill Peel, Michael Freemantle

1

2

3

Photo: Flickr user moriza

37 Marks and Meaning

According to *Psychology Today,* each of us is subjected to anywhere between 3,000 and 10,000 brand exposures every day. We don't yet understand the complete psychological effect of so many commercial messages, but this much is clear: Logos play a big part in this increasingly rich and complex landscape.

Graphic identities and the entities they represent need to reflect the values, demographics, and psychology of their intended audience. Many essential elements of a graphic identity—shape, color, pattern, etc.—mean different things to different audiences. Understanding people's needs and desires through research and rapid prototyping is one way of evaluating graphic treatments for an identity. Can you test the appeal and connotation of a red logo in South Korea vs. Western Europe? Another method involves consideration of trends and the competitive landscape. What ideas are being adopted from another culture? Is Hello Kitty on the rise for your target audience?

Understanding users and the context of use informs the development of graphic identities that delivers the desired effect.

Who wants to wear this shirt? How about those mittens? Whether you do or don't, what does that say about you? To what type of person do these marks appeal?

1

1. BEAST Streetwear
BEAST Strategic Branding & Graphic Design
Jeremy Thompson

2. Zilar
Natoof
Mariam bin Natoof

3. Mäser Austria
Simon & Goetz Design GmbH & Co. KG
Gerrit Hinkelbein

4. Over the Moon
The Creative Method
Tony Ibbotson, Andi Yanto

5. Ruby et Violette
The O Group
Jason B. Cohen, Marites Algones

2

over the moon

3

4

5

38 Program Context

As a graphic identity moves into the physical world and interacts with spaces and objects over time, often the audience experiences a more visceral and immediate effect.

As you enter a retail store, do you pass through glass doors? Do the interior graphics entice you to look up or down? Does the space remind you of your garage or kitchen?

Do the photos in a brochure encourage close examination or a cursory glance? Does the text make you want to read it twice? Does the printed piece look like a phone book or a work of art?

The application of program elements can be a powerful way of amplifying the psychological effect of the graphic identity.

Dedeman
Brandient
Cristian "Kit" Paul, Iancu Barbarasa

From product packaging to selling environments, there's a time for soft and subtle and a place for bold and direct.

amala
Liska + Associates
Tanya Quick, Jenn Cash

39 Brand Psychology

The world's most memorable brands tend to distinguish themselves in the connotation—not just the denotation—of the value proposition. Brand builders strive to create just the right connotation for the brand in the mind of its target audience. Success in this endeavor is a rare and precious commodity.

While the idea of corporate reputation is nothing new among public relations and marketing professionals, linking diverse brand initiatives for a cumulative psychological effect on target audiences is the work of building a brand identity. It starts and ends with what people think—or, more accurately, what a brand can inspire people to think.

1

2

3

Most people don't know enough about wine to make educated purchases. Fortunately, wine distributors know a lot about people and they know how to craft packaging to capture the attention of wine consumers.

1. Fire Road
2. Saint Clair
3. Ti Amo
4. Marlborough Sun
The Creative Method
Tony Ibbotson, Andi Yanto, Mayra Monobe

4

40 Idea Generation

Trying to define the logo design process is a little like trying to answer the question, "How long does it take to come up with a good idea?" Some designers wrestle with a graphic identity project for a year or more. Others leave the first client meeting with a workable solution in mind.

While the timeline can be unpredictable, good designers learn to trust the creative process. Generally, this process starts with an understanding of the vision and context for the project. Next, it draws upon ideation techniques taught in design school: research, goal-oriented creative briefs, prototyping, and other innovation methods. Testing and refinement follow.

Generating a lot of ideas throughout the process can be a good way to arrive at a great solution, but volume does not guarantee quality. Developing a good set of filters for editing your ideas is an essential step for creating an effective graphic identity.

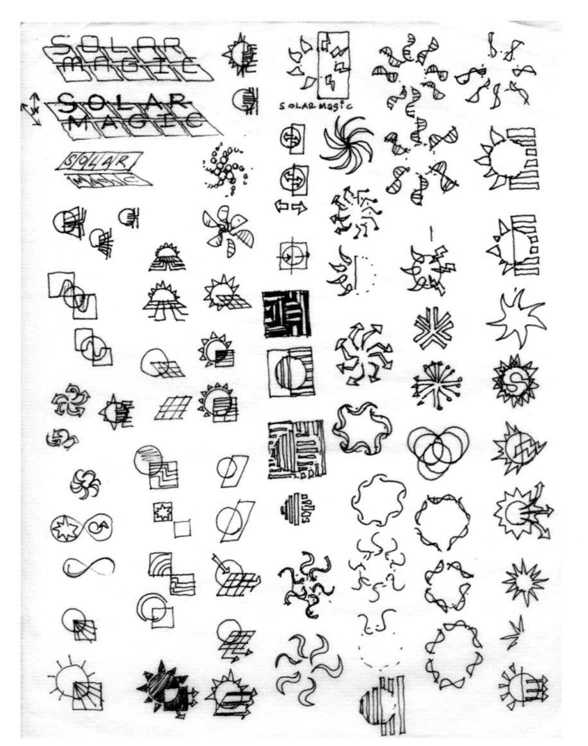

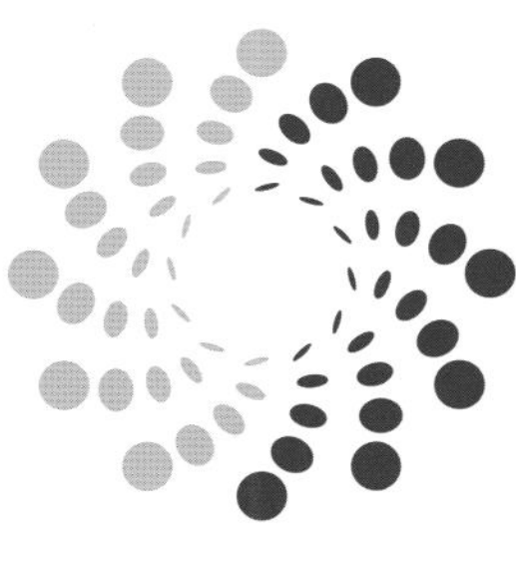

National Semiconductor SolarMagic Logo
Gee + Chung Design
Earl Gee

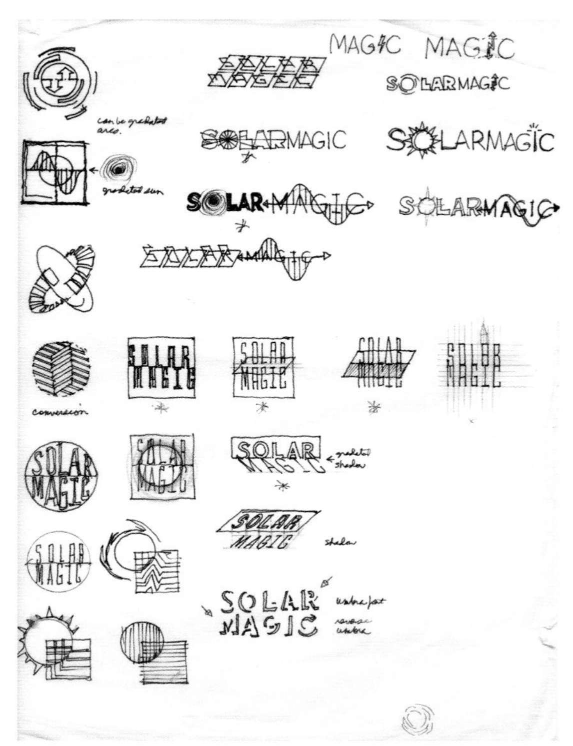

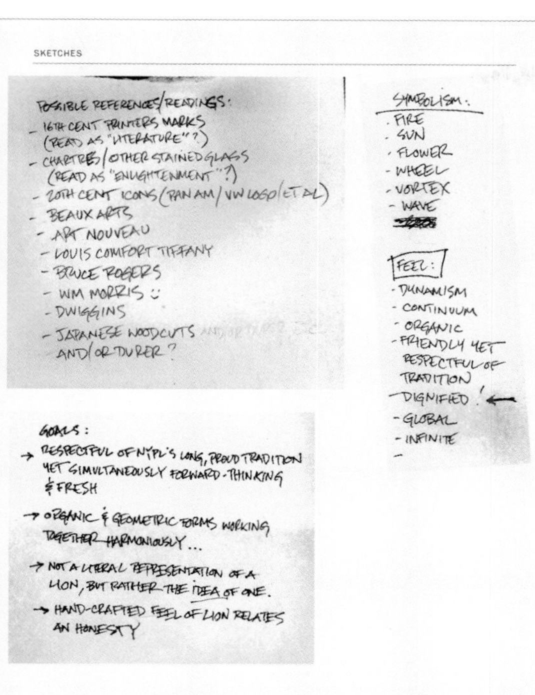

New York Public Library
New York Public Library
Graphic Design Office
Marc Blaustein

All the marvels of computer-aided graphics aside, there is no substitute for the napkin sketch.

41 Prototyping

Creating an identity program starts with understanding its context: Where does the identity need to manifest itself? Who is using it, and why? Context determines media options, and the combination of media constraints, business objectives, and program elements provide valuable input for prototyping.

The program is the rubber-meets-the-road moment when the theories are tested out. Prototyping plays a key role in the program development process. The program may undergo more iterative phases than the logo. Visualizing potential solutions can be a very useful way to evaluate the effectiveness of individual ideas. The goal is to fail fast and learn through testing and evaluation.

Courtesy: People Design

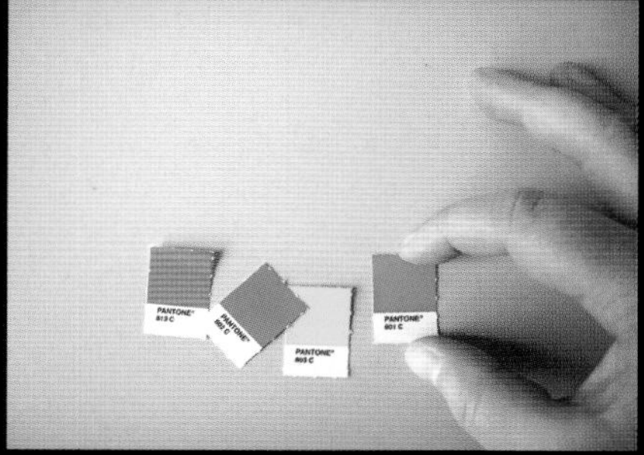

Generating a lot of options during a prototyping phase can be an effective way to quickly test out ideas before a large investment is made.

42 Strategic Foundations

It's easier to create a brand identity on paper than it is to put it into practice. Making the brand promise is one thing. Keeping it is quite another.

Potential customers identify a brand by its artifacts as well as its actions. It makes sense, then, that the process of building brand identity typically begins with an exploration of these artifacts: the graphic identity and program elements. But it quickly goes much deeper. Brand identity work warrants frank, strategic business conversations about an organization's value proposition and positioning. A solid understanding of the business strategy will result in a brand identity that supports the strategic direction of the business.

Once a business foundation is in place, other important human factors play a role in the brand identity, including the character of the company, its audiences, and the marketplace. Through the iterative process, designers often land on a better understanding of the meaning and values of the brand. Often, the work of building the brand helps to actualize the brand attributes.

PROBLEM FRAMING

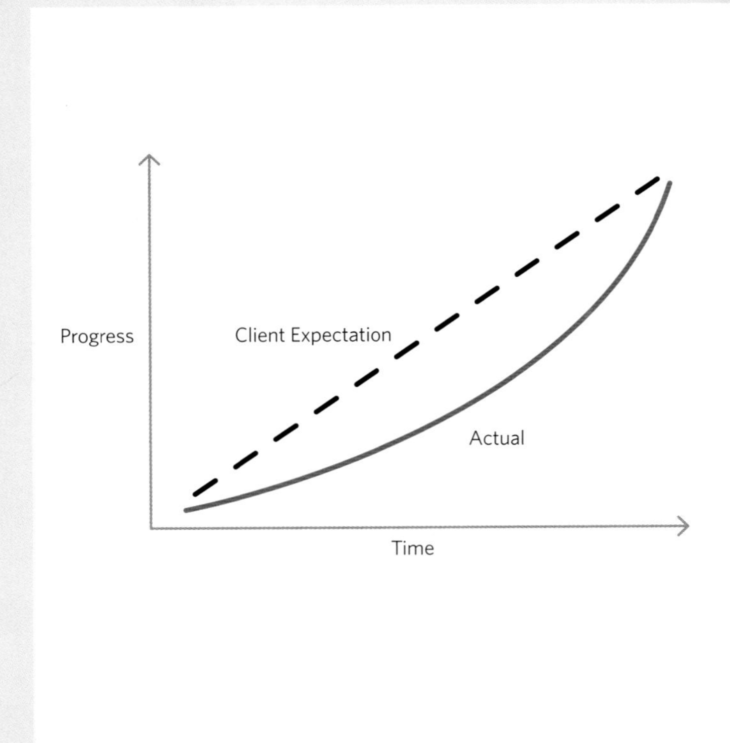

Front-loaded with research and strategy formulation, the design process sometimes takes time before resulting in work that can be easily recognized as progress.

Courtesy: Jeremy Alexis, Matt Bebee, IIT Institute of Design

DESIGN PROCESS

Defining the Problem

1 Defining the problem

2 Envisioning the desired end state

3 Defining the approach

4 Inciting support and then action

Innovating

5 Seeking insight

6 Prototyping potential solutions

7 Delineating the tough choices

8 Enabling the team

Generating Value

9 Choosing the best solution

10 Communicating the solution

11 Selling the solution

12 Learning and tracking

A solid but flexible work process yields better results. AIGA endorses this process, which maps a commonsensical approach to strategic problem solving.

Courtesy: AIGA

43 Production Methods

Graphic identity design has its roots in offset lithography, and the constraints of printing technology have influenced the form and character of logos. Simple, easy-to-reproduce shapes have been the standard for logos since the 1960s. As printing technology has advanced, however, the constraints have loosened.

Digital imaging technology has opened many doors, allowing for color logo application on a variety of substrates and materials, loosening typically conservative application standards. While it remains prudent to consider the worst-case-scenario application when developing a graphic identity, the worst-case-scenario production method often isn't so bad anymore.

While some designers debate the merits of new methods over traditional techniques, others have taken advantage of these changes by creating graphic identities with characteristics previously avoided: multiple colors, complex shapes, gradients, and fine lines.

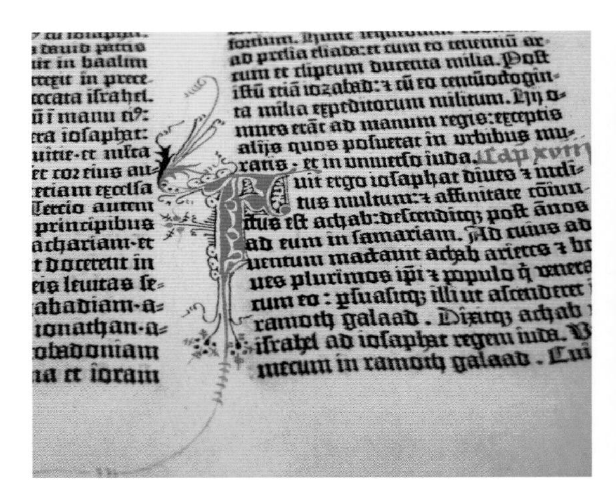

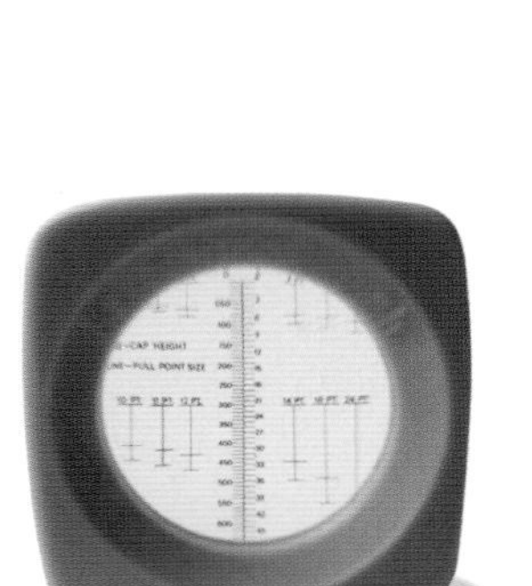

From the Guttenberg Bible to modern moveable type, production tools and methods shape identity artifacts.

Photo: Jeremy Frechette

Photos: Flickr users Kelly McCarthy, wilhei

Digital technology has created new opportunities for new styles of graphic identity design.

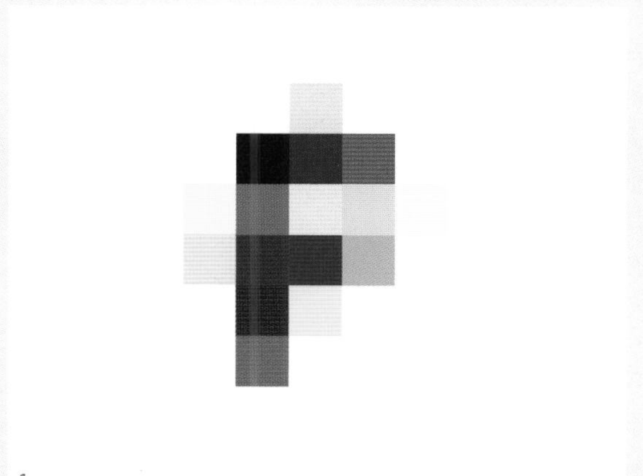
1

2

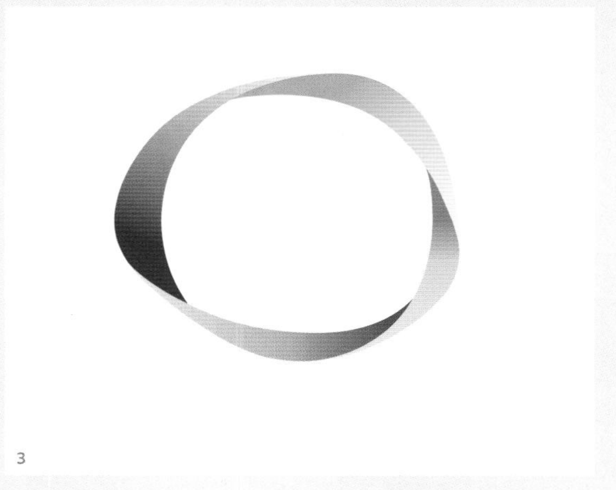
3

4

5

6

1. Freedom Film Festival
Organic Grid
Michael McDonald

2. Vocii
Tandemodus
Kelly Komp, Andy Eltzroth, Charee Klimek, Classic Color, Bill Borque

3. Cambridge
samatamason
Kevin Krueger, Skot Waldron, Jason Schifferer

4. Singularity University
MINE™
Christopher Simmons, Tim Belonax

5. Phoenix House
Siegel+Gale
Sven Seger, Doug Sellers, Lana Roulhac, Hayley Berlent

6. UMW
Lippincott
Vincenzo Perri, Bogdan Geana

44 "Image" as a Verb

New imaging and production techniques have thrown the doors wide open for identity programs. From wrapped buildings and vehicles to backlit projections and temporary tattoos, opportunities for creative surface treatments for identities abound.

Graphic identity design has advanced along with technology, inspiring some designers to create graphically complex marks, some of which blur the line between illustrative logos and illustrations. Remember not to jettison clarity and legibility to make way for creative complexity. Often, a more intricate mark requires a simpler application, while a more straightforward mark can lend itself to busier applications.

Even though there are new production techniques, basic design principles remain constant. The goal remains to evolve a distinctive identity into an effective program. Identity programs have constraints based on audience appropriateness and strategic alignment with brand objectives. Be informed and inspired by new production options for identity programs as they arise, but don't be too driven by them.

1

5 Benefits of Digital Printing

SOURCE
Bruce Hansen
A veteran of 40 years in the printing industry

Printing aficionados might cringe at the thought, but the days of hot type are over. Digital technology has affected every aspect of the printing industry—and it's here to stay. While the quality of digital printing may never possess the old-fashioned craftsmanship of traditional methods, it can benefit designers and design buyers in a number of ways.

1. Timeliness
Speed is improving rapidly. A printing project that would have required a six-week process in 2007 can be done in a week and a half in 2010.

2. Proofing
Back when the industry was working in analog, no two proofs looked the same. Today, the digital process not only means more consistent proofs, but also the opportunity to find and fix more mistakes.

3. Reproofing
Not long ago, if you were on press and discovered a problem with photography, it would have added a week to the printing schedule. Now you can retouch it and reproof it on the fly.

4. Print on demand
Many companies are moving to print on demand. By posting a file in PDF format, they can allow their clients to select prescripted pages and prescripted photos, and print their own small quantities of the project. The quality will suffer, but the cost savings will continue to prompt companies to go with this option.

5. Lower expectations
"Good enough" satisfies 99 percent of the people 99 percent of the time. Designers might be able to tell the difference between a project printed digitally and a project printed with traditional production methods, but if the difference is imperceptible to the audience for a piece, is it worth investing the time and money necessary to get it perfect?

1. Abaltat
Detail. Design Studio

2. Kingfisher Plumbing
Spring Advertising
Perry Chua, Shon Tanner, Sami Christianson

3. Sandy Leong
The O Group
Jason B. Cohen, J. Kenneth Rothermich

4. Atelier LaDurance
StormHand
Boy Bastiaens

5. Community Foundation of Greater Chattanooga
Maycreate
Brian May, Monty Wyne, Chris Enter

6. Herman Miller ICFF
People Design

2

Spongy business cards, four-color billboards, laser-precision diecuts: It's all on the table with today's production technology.

3

4

5

6

45 New Sources of Meaning

At the highest level, design is the creation or assembly of elements into a cohesive, meaningful order. The emergence of new elements creates opportunities for new meaning—and that's what innovation is all about.

The production landscape inevitably shapes brands as innovative firms and designers leverage new techniques—often to solve old problems in new and different ways. Midcentury design icons Charles and Ray Eames capitalized on the then emerging technique of plywood molding in their furniture designs for Herman Miller. While molded plywood wasn't the core problem, it presented an opportunity that led the Herman Miller brand into the modern furniture landscape—and left it forever changed.

New production techniques influence brands in small ways all the time. You have to design with end production methods in mind, and keep an eye out for advances in order to take full advantage of them.

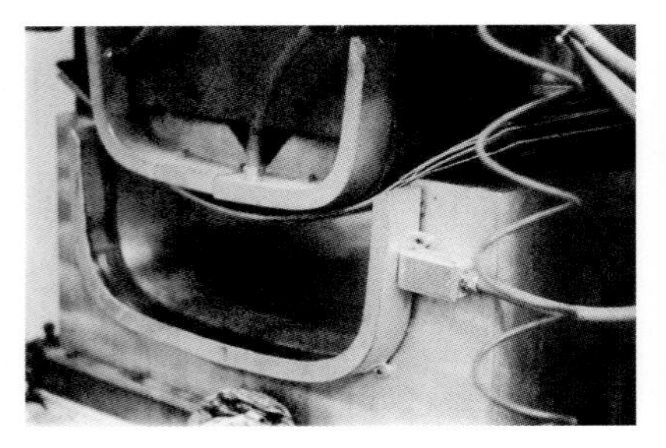

Courtesy: Herman Miller, Inc.

New production methods sometimes lead designers and brands in new directions. Charles and Ray Eames moved furniture company Herman Miller to the forefront of modern design by making beautiful use of plywood molding techniques. Textile design firm Studio Z combined patented Jacqform™ weaving technology with laser cutting to create these unique gadget bags.

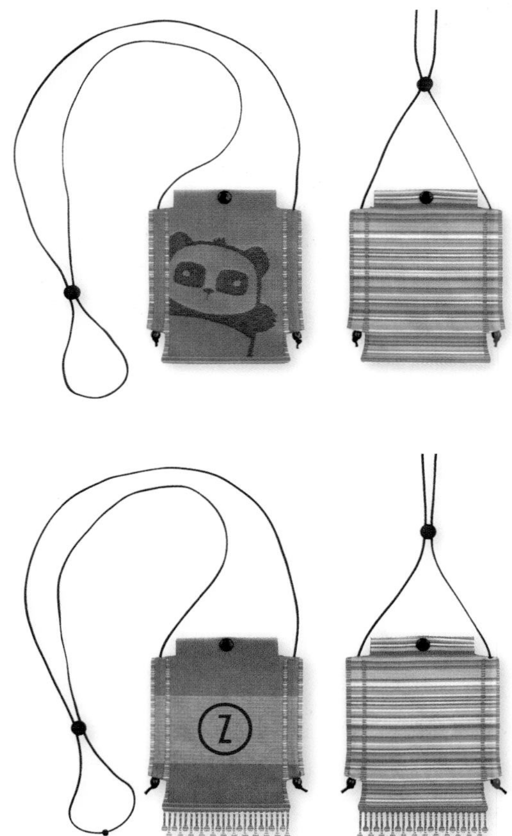

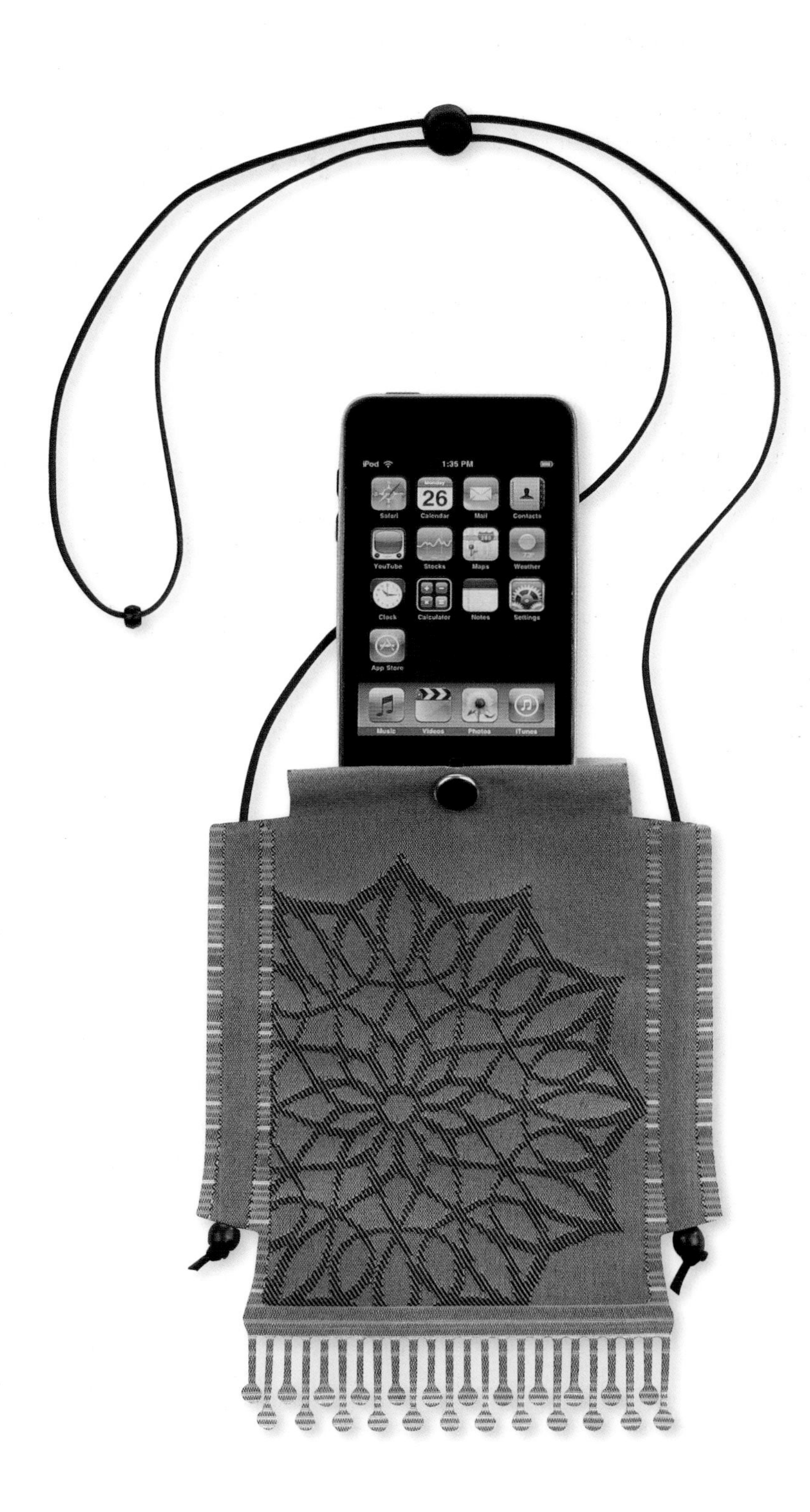

Courtesy: Studio Z

46 Pictures in Pixels

Seismic shifts in communications technology are rapidly transforming graphic identity design. The brave new digital world has given rise to the concept of digital identity.

Simply put, digital identities bring graphic identities into digital spaces. However, this new landscape is vast, and navigating it requires both traditional design sense and technological savvy.

As graphic identities move into a digital context, designers will encounter some notable differences. Print on paper offers high resolution, but low color depth (typically only two to six inks, with solids and halftone screens). Digital displays, on the other hand, offer relatively low resolution but high depth of color (RGB used in millions of color combinations). Instead of simple line art shapes or screens of halftone dots, digital devices display pixels—square "picture elements"—to create images. Out are clean, sharp graphics; in are softer, pixilated (antialiased) edges.

Graphic identities in digital spaces present new opportunities—more colors available in more places—and new constraints, such as the problem of creating a nice-looking image in a 16-by-16 pixel favicon.

Bags
Push
Chris Robb, Mark Unger, Forest Young

Large and small companies alike are dealing with the new constraints and opportunities of digital graphic identity.

Google

Google™

Courtesy: Google

47 Building an Online Identity

Digital media offer vast, new opportunities for identity programs. There is a dizzying array of new choices, and they seem to be changing all the time.

HTML, CSS, JavaScript, Flash, video, sound, animation, and web graphics are the tools of the early twenty-first century user interface designer. Don't try to be an expert in all areas. Strive for a working knowledge of the emerging digital landscape and commit to ongoing research in order to keep up.

Smart phones and social media are opening up new avenues for online identity programs. Know that basic design principles are as relevant in Facebook and Twitter as they are for a product or package.

1

User experience design is a relatively young, but rapidly evolving, field with tremendous implications on the future of digital program design.

2

3

4

5

6

7

8

9

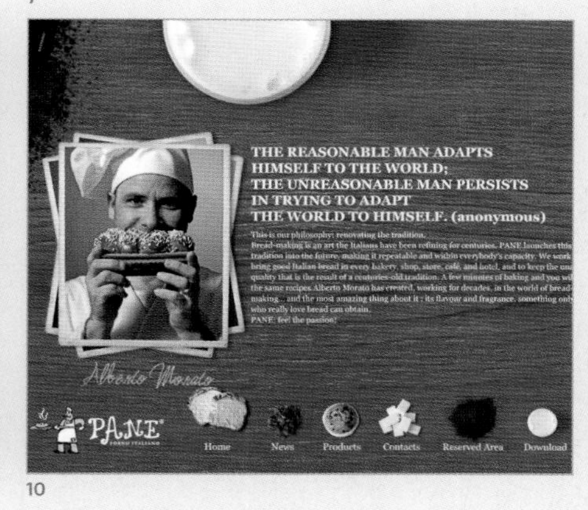

10

1. Loose Collective
G-MAN

2. Bloomscape
People Design

3. Proces 15
Bunch

4. From the Desk of Lola
still room
Jessica Fleischmann

5. Cumberland Furniture
People Design

6. Sweet Dreams
The Creative Method
Tony Ibbotson

7. Creative Byline
People Design

8. Workamajig
Push
Chris Robb, Mark Unger, Forest Young

9. American Numismatic Society
Piscatello Design Centre
Rocco Piscatello, Junno Hamaguchi

10. Pane Srl
Ad Grafica & Comunicazione
Giancarlo Salvador, Gianpiero Surico

48 Digital Brands

It's been said that half the money in advertising is wasted, but the trick is figuring out which half—a problem online advertisers have endeavored to solve.

Progressive firms will be targeted but aggressive in building digital brands, taking opportunities to experiment with new models, to fail fast, and to stay agile enough to react to changing conditions.

There is clearly fertile ground in the identity elements such as motion, time, and sound. The opportunity for innovation is too large to overlook. In the future, digital brand identities will be less about any specific artifact or brand control, and more about inclusion, affinity, and the entire customer experience envelope.

1

2

Identity designers must continue to expand their knowledge and skills to meet the evolving challenges of the digital media landscape.

1. Artificio
Gabriela Soto Grant

2. TextaChef
Designfox Interactive
Martin liu

3. T-HT Award
Bunch

3

49 Logo Trends

Creating a new graphic identity can be an expensive endeavor. When organizations commit to such an investment, they typically don't see it as fleeting or frivolous. Nevertheless, one can't discount the influence of trends—from the worlds of art, fashion, technology, etc.—on identity design.

New companies have the luxury of starting with a blank piece of paper, crafting from scratch an identity that reflects current sensibilities, from typefaces to colors. This can put pressure on firms with a longer history, which could feel pressure to update an established graphic identity to appear more current.

Trends come from trendsetters. Keep this in mind. Would you rather be Nike or one of the countless other companies that felt compelled to add a "swoosh" to their logos during the 1990s? Because trends are fleeting, copying a trendsetter is ill advised—unless being a fast follower is part of an organization's explicit strategy.

Curvy

1

2

3

Designers don't work in a bubble, so the influence of trends on graphic identity design can't be completely avoided.

1. Ramanauskas & Partners
LOOVVOOL
Hannes Unt, Kadri-Maria Mitt, Valter Kaleta

2. ArtServe
Square One Design
Mike Gorman, Lindsay Jones

3. Aquarius Advisers
John Langdon Design

4. Curzon Cinemas
Subtitle.
Michael Salu

5. matter
Pentagram
Angus Hyland, William Russell

6. Michael & Susan Dell Foundation
Obnocktious
Tia Primova, Brandon Payton

7. Arealis
LOOVVOOL
Hannes Unt, Robi Jõeleht, Valter Kaleta

8. Setterholm Productions
Wink
Scott Thares, Richard Boynton

9. Atlanta Film & Video
Fitzgerald+CO/Deep Design
Heath Beeferman, Rick Grimsley

Brackets

[CURZON • CINEMAS]

4

matter

5

Spirograph

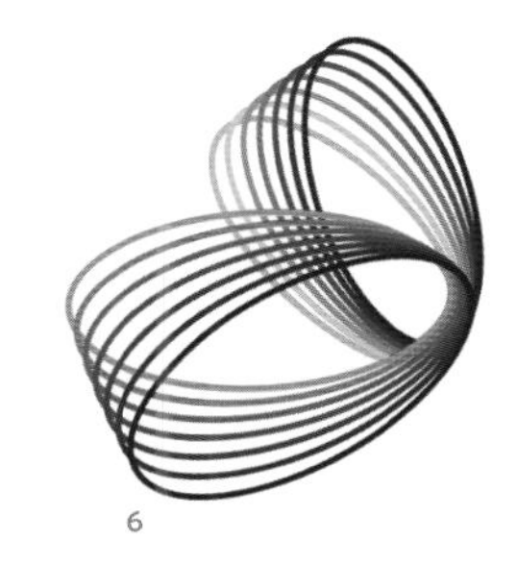

6

7

3-D

8

9

50 Popular Culture

Since identity programs change with some frequency, they can reflect popular culture more easily than graphic identities. It's generally not a good idea to change either one too frequently, but refreshed graphics, colors, and other program elements can keep an identity program relevant.

Program designers do their work in a big, diverse world. For example, macro trends sparked by new production techniques or the mainstreaming of sustainability undeniably influence that work. When designing an identity program, you have a choice: Either recognize the impact of current macro trends on the industry and respond in a carefully measured way, or follow in lock step. Choose the latter, and the result may be a lack of consistency in the program over time.

Seasonal or market trends penetrate a culture in a much shallower way, but their fleeting influence can be important to some organizations. Allowing a program the flexibility to react to seasonal or market trends starts with a clear understanding of what remains constant about the organization's brand identity. Following trends too closely might diminish what you've built. Being recognizable and unique usually delivers greater brand equity than being trendy. Brands that are explicitly focused on trend provide the exception, but these organizations are also more likely to be trendsetters, rather than followers.

What led these churches to need a rebrand?

Warehouse 242
Eye Design Studio
Gage Mitchell, Chris Bradle, Steve Whitby

Tenth Church
Nancy Wu Design

51 Macro Trends

Macro trends in brand identity are tied to trends in business models and lifestyles.

Consider the rise of the McDonald's brand and the value proposition of easily accessible, inexpensive fast food. Beginning with its founding in 1948, McDonald's developed a breakthrough business model that many other restaurant chains copied. As such, it helped define a category.

McDonald's brand identity remained successful for decades, but has been challenged in recent years by industry rivals such as Subway, which built a new brand around healthier lifestyle trends. Similarly, the rise of Starbucks Coffee Company reflects a set of brand characteristics that center on food quality and a sense of community. Neither Subway nor Starbucks could have existed without McDonald's before them. Likewise, from menu variety to store design, the experience of a McDonald's restaurant anywhere in the world today has been shaped in part by macro trends that Subway and Starbucks capitalized on first.

All living brands react to macro trends—and yes, no reaction is a type of reaction. The most effective brands translate these trends into meaning, and deliver more meaningful experiences to customers as a result.

The drive-thru experience.

Photos: Flickr users AchimH, thetruthabout

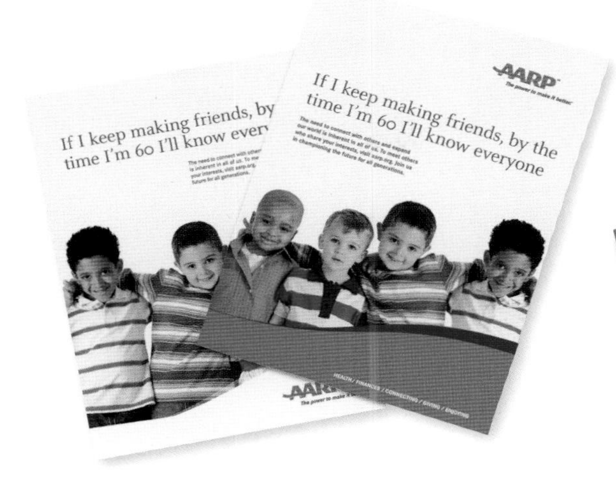

AARP no longer targets retired people exclusively, and no longer does the organization see its name as an acronym (it formerly stood for the American Association of Retired Persons). The brand is a trendsetter in the United States, with great influence on how older Americans view themselves.

AARP
Siegel+Gale
Howard Belk, Anne Swan, Clinton Clarke, Steve Kim, Lana Roulhac, Frank Oswald, Jenifer Brooks, Hayley Berlent

52 Do the Right Thing

The tools for graphic design have never been less expensive or more readily available than they are now. If you trace the path from hand-lettered texts to the Gutenberg Bible to large-scale commercial printing to desktop publishing, never before have such cheap tools for graphic design found their way into the hands of so many potential designers.

Graphic identity is a touchstone for the industry, and logos are among the most tangible artifacts graphic designers produce. Today, anyone with a computer and Internet access can create a kind of graphic identity—and many try. Thanks to clip art, online logo generators, and business models based on crowdsourcing, logos are abundant and, well, cheap.

On the surface, cheaply produced logos appeal to some organizations. A brand manager may feel great about getting away with a $99 (£64) logo, but would she feel just as good after applying that $99 (£64) logo to tens of thousands of dollars worth of magazine ads, delivery trucks, business cards, lobby signs, etc.? Is it something the organization wants to live with for the next decade? Moreover, does the logo accurately represent what the organization stands for?

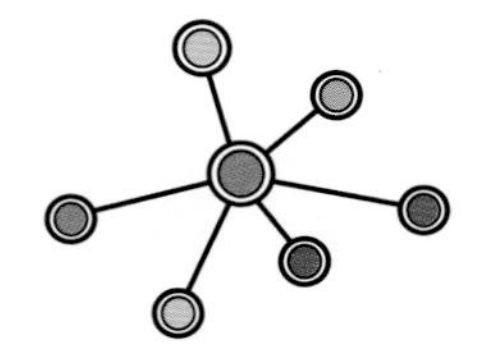

"Synergy"

"Humanist"

"Dotcom"

Source: Vista Print

Online logo generators can produce logos cheaply—in the case of these logos, less than 200 bucks (£130). But more often than not, you get what you pay for.

"Navigator"

"Aerospace"

"Global"

"Growth"

"Three Principles"

"Peak"

53 Program Investments

Economics drive every decision to adopt a cheaply produced logo. The good news for identity program designers is that they also can benefit from new money-saving techniques.

Cost efficiency in program design results from proactively investigating program patterns and elements, and understanding how graphic identities should manifest themselves in application. Create artifacts worth having, but look for ways to reduce cost by planning ahead to avoid having to reinvent the wheel.

Based on volume alone, it'd be easy to short-change the budget of a graphic identity and spend more on various program elements. While it's true that over time, organizations typically spend much more money on identity programs, the most cost-efficient programs are built from solid graphic identities. In fact, the motive for reinvention late in the production cycle is often due to a lack of depth in the initial graphic identity. Designers can help their clients save money over the long run by investing a little more up front.

TACA
Lippincott
Rodney Abbot, Rodney Abbot, Sam Ayling, Steve Lawrence

Once you commit to a good mark, commit to using it purposefully to maximize your investment.

The Legal Aid Society
Siegel+Gale
Sven Seger, Doug Sellers, Jong Woo Si, Jenifer Brooks

54 Walk the Talk

Whether an organization invests up front in its graphic identity, or gets away with a cheap logo and carelessly slaps it on everything possible, a strong brand identity is hard to fake.

Brand identity taps into what an organization does, how it behaves, or who it is—or is trying to become. The graphic identity and identity program exist to enhance or describe the brand identity. They should all add up to a coherent whole. This takes work, practice, expertise, trial and error, and perseverance.

Everyone understands the importance of being frugal. Whether an investment is advisable or wasteful changes by audience or market. What remains constant is the need for organizations to have a sense of self as they make financial and operational decisions about their identity. A company's actions must match its words. If they don't, every dollar spent to communicate its brand promise has been wasted.

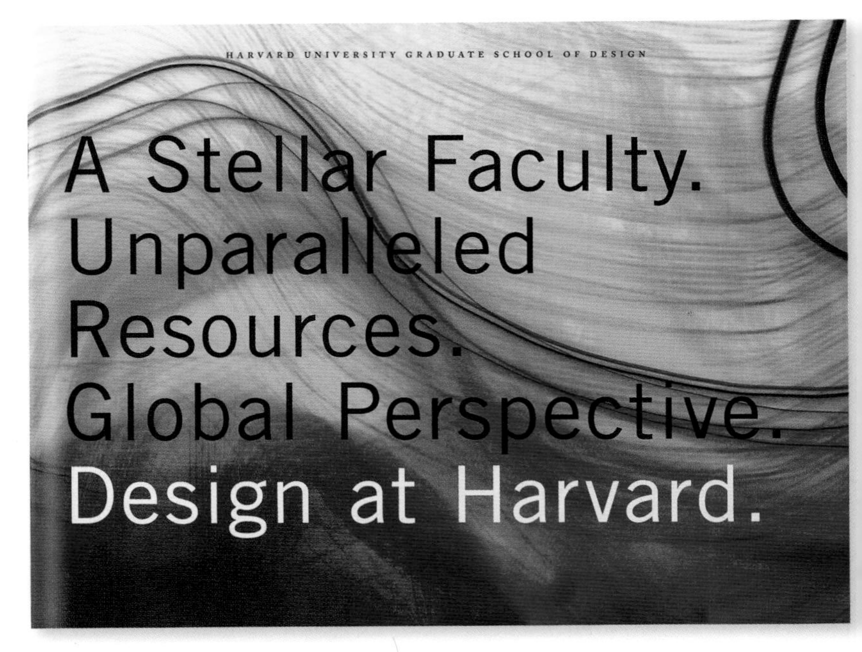

Don't say you have unparalleled resources and a global perspective unless you do. Of course, it's very likely that Harvard does, but beware of hyperbole.

Harvard Design School
Hahn Smith Design
Nigel Smith, Alison Hahn, Sara Soskolne

Summer 1997
Harvard Design Magazine
Look
Again
Recognizing neglected design
$7 US

Winter/Spring 1997
Harvard Design Magazine
Changing
Cities
plus
The New Urbanism
Gender and Design

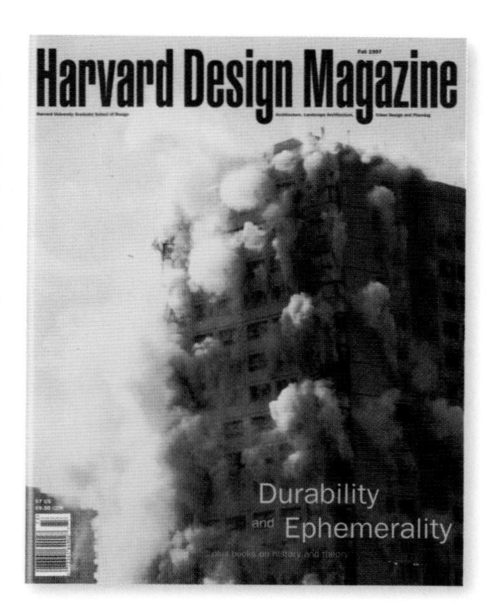
Fall 1997
Harvard Design Magazine
Durability
and Ephemerality

Still Here

Green Chaos

carlos jiménez: house and studio

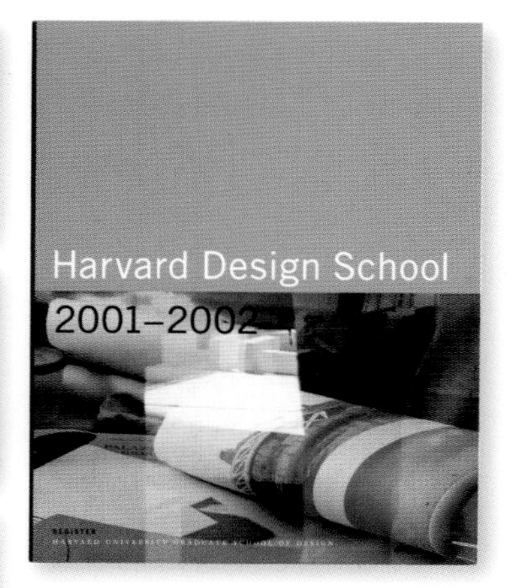
Harvard Design School
2001–2002

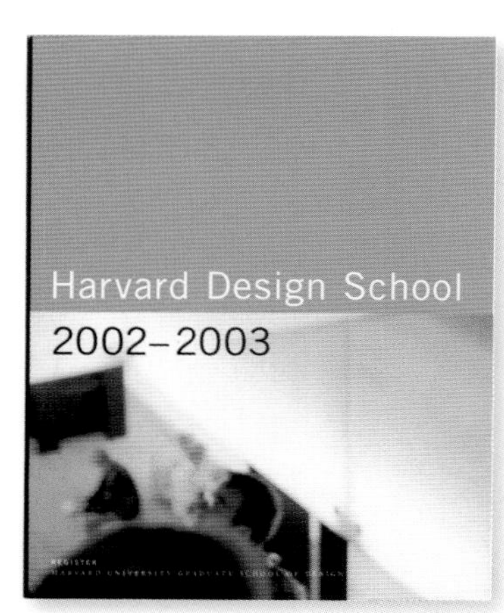
Harvard Design School
2002–2003

55 New Interactions

Remember what life was like before Facebook? It doesn't really matter whether you do or not. Those days are gone, and they're not coming back.

The ways in which companies interact with their customers have changed forever thanks to social media. Exactly what kind of impact social media will have on graphic identity design has yet to be determined. Preliminary indications point to a significant impact, one in which do-it-yourself tools allow customers to create and protect their own identities in spaces where they commingle with the graphic identities of companies large and small. On Twitter, Facebook, or any social networking site, who's to say a company's graphic identity has any more influence than an individual bloggers' graphic identity?

Organizations will need to consider how their brands—as represented by their graphic identities—translate into these new channels. A focus on consistency and clarity is warranted. More importantly, designers can encourage organizations with whom they work to stay open to learning about the new constraints and opportunities presented by social media as they arise.

The world of social media is flat, where corporate graphic identities and the identities of their customers inhabit the same spaces.

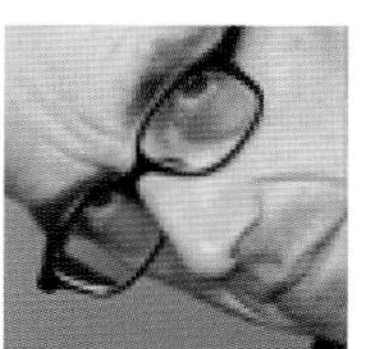

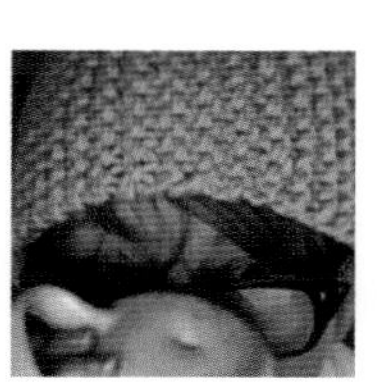

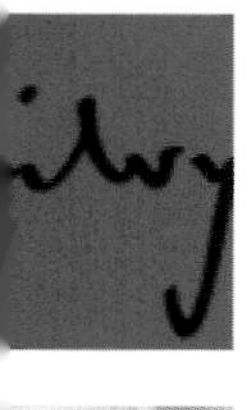
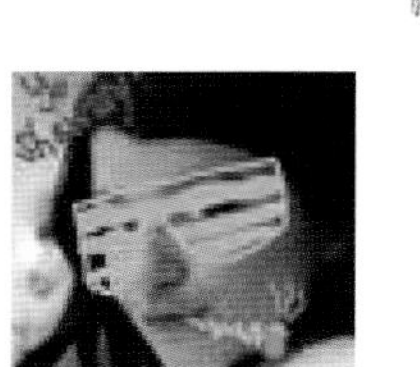

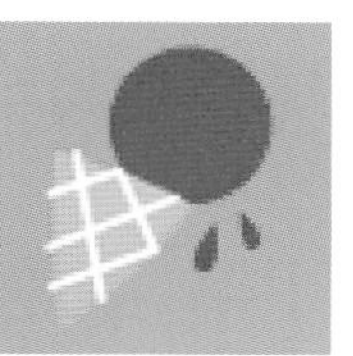

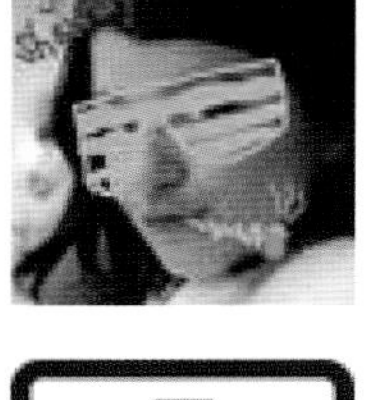

56 Social Innovation

New media are continually offering new opportunities for identity programs. Many of these avenues present wonderful options for gaining customer mindshare and loyalty. Social media in particular is ripe with new places for innovation.

These tools—and the customers using them—are changing rapidly. As organizations venture into the social media landscape, they need to have a greater willingness to learn and experiment than they may have allowed with other media. Adopting the mantra of Web 2.0 software developers, "failing fast" is a good way to think about progress here. The winners on this new frontier will need to take some risks. At the same time, consider how other program materials interact with social media materials, and how traditional program elements work in these new environments.

Program designers and managers need to stay informed about these options, but also understand how they comprise only a part of the overall customer experience—and for now, only a segment of their customer audience. It's a segment that's growing rapidly, however, and likely to ultimately change the overall brand experience landscape.

New program opportunities mean having to plan for Facebook, Twitter, and whatever platform comes next. Online content is increasingly user-generated.

1

1. **Spout**
2. **Whirlpool Unleashing Innovation**
People Design

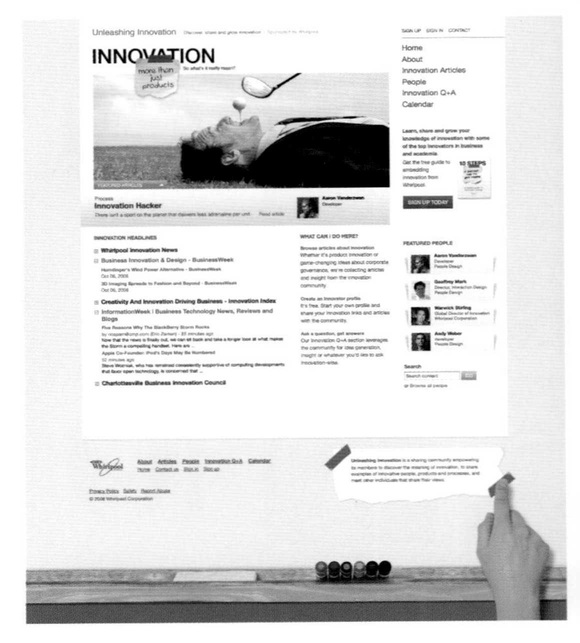

2

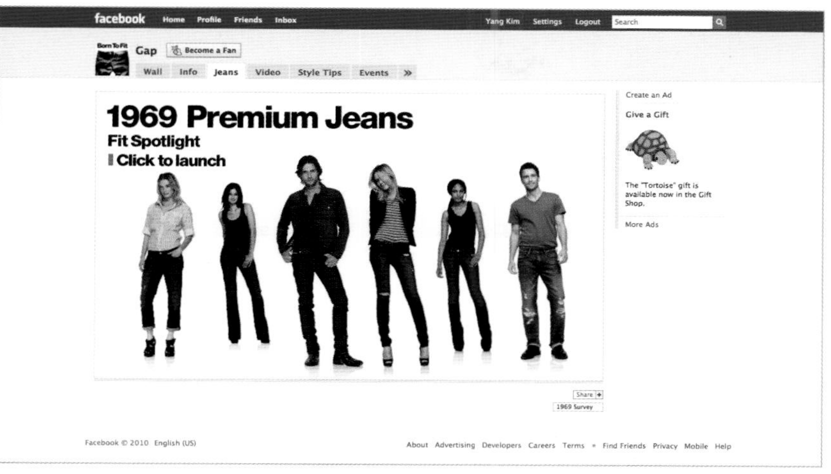
facebook
Home Profile Friends Inbox
Yang Kim Settings Logout
Gap
Become a Fan
Wall Info Jeans Video Style Tips Events
1969 Premium Jeans
Fit Spotlight
Click to launch
Create an Ad
Give a Gift
The "Tortoise" gift is available now in the Gift Shop.
More Ads
Facebook © 2010 English (US)
About Advertising Developers Careers Terms Find Friends Privacy Mobile Help

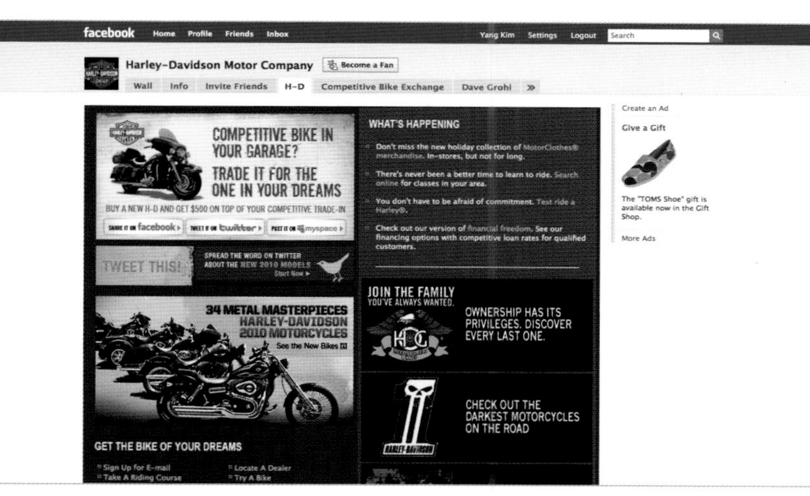
facebook
Home Profile Friends Inbox
Yang Kim Settings Logout
Harley-Davidson Motor Company
Become a Fan
Wall Info Invite Friends H-D Competitive Bike Exchange Dave Grohl
COMPETITIVE BIKE IN YOUR GARAGE?
TRADE IT FOR THE ONE IN YOUR DREAMS
TWEET THIS!
34 METAL MASTERPIECES
HARLEY-DAVIDSON
2010 MOTORCYCLES
GET THE BIKE OF YOUR DREAMS
WHAT'S HAPPENING
JOIN THE FAMILY
OWNERSHIP HAS ITS PRIVILEGES. DISCOVER EVERY LAST ONE.
CHECK OUT THE DARKEST MOTORCYCLES ON THE ROAD
Create an Ad
Give a Gift
The "TOMS Shoe" gift is available now in the Gift Shop.
More Ads

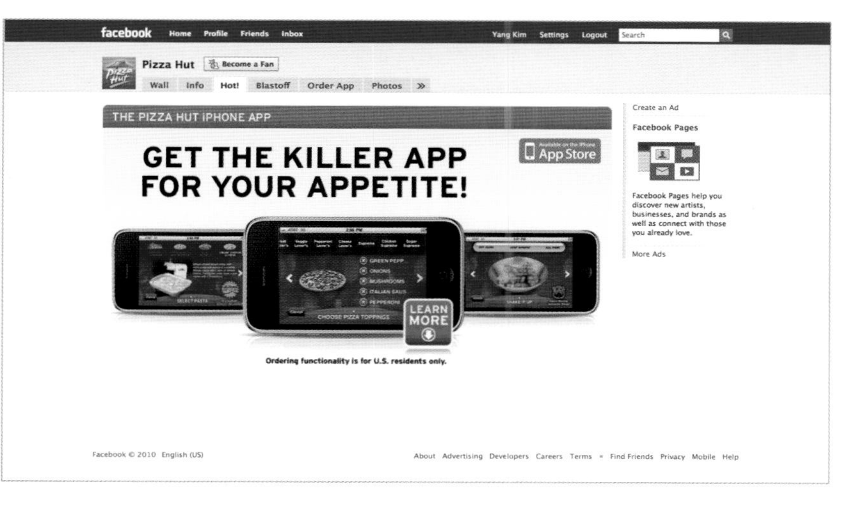
facebook
Home Profile Friends Inbox
Yang Kim Settings Logout
Pizza Hut
Become a Fan
Wall Info Hot! Blastoff Order App Photos
THE PIZZA HUT IPHONE APP
GET THE KILLER APP FOR YOUR APPETITE!
App Store
LEARN MORE
Ordering functionality is for U.S. residents only.
Create an Ad
Facebook Pages
Facebook Pages help you discover new artists, businesses, and brands as well as connect with those you already love.
More Ads
Facebook © 2010 English (US)
About Advertising Developers Careers Terms Find Friends Privacy Mobile Help

twitter
peopledesign
I posted 4 photos on Facebook in the album "Friday, February 5, 2010" http://bit.ly/dorxXD

twitter
ladygaga
http://twitpic.com/11firi - beautiful photo taken of me the moment I found out i won my grammys. All the hundreds of songs I wrote, the thou

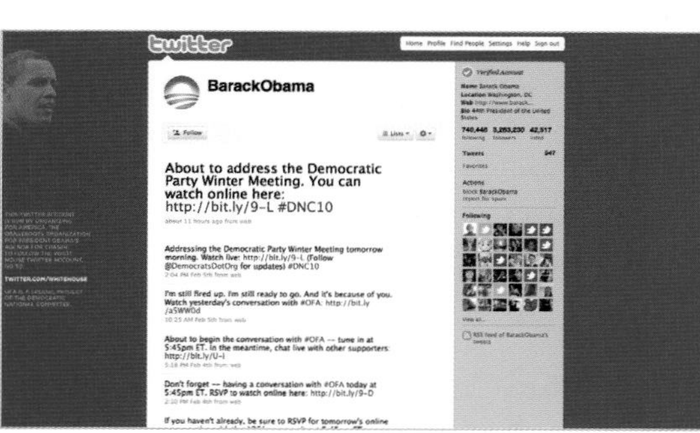
twitter
BarackObama
About to address the Democratic Party Winter Meeting. You can watch online here: http://bit.ly/9-L #DNC10

twitter
aplusk
@koreelove nice catch
NO LOITERING

57 Transparent Brands

Entering the social media landscape means understanding how a company should interact in a social environment—on a deeper level than what the logo looks like on Twitter. In a crowd of individuals, how does a company hold up in terms of social relevance? Is it a wallflower or the life of the party?

We'd submit that half of what goes on today in the brave, new world of social media could be characterized as an experiment. The trick might be recognizing that the other half will likely change the world.

In this area, companies need even more diligence about clearly conveying intent, being genuine, and not overpromising. Slip up in any of these areas, and the social consequences can be detrimental to a brand reputation—and hard to correct.

THEN

In the old communication model, many interactions were not captured.

Brand

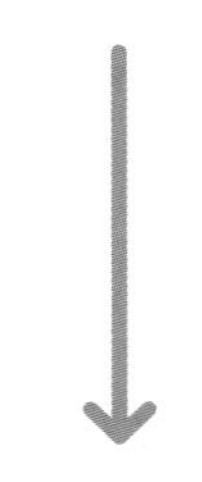

Customer

NOW

The social media model creates digital links between groups of people. Many of these links existed already; now that they're quantifiable, what opportunities do they represent for brands?

Brand

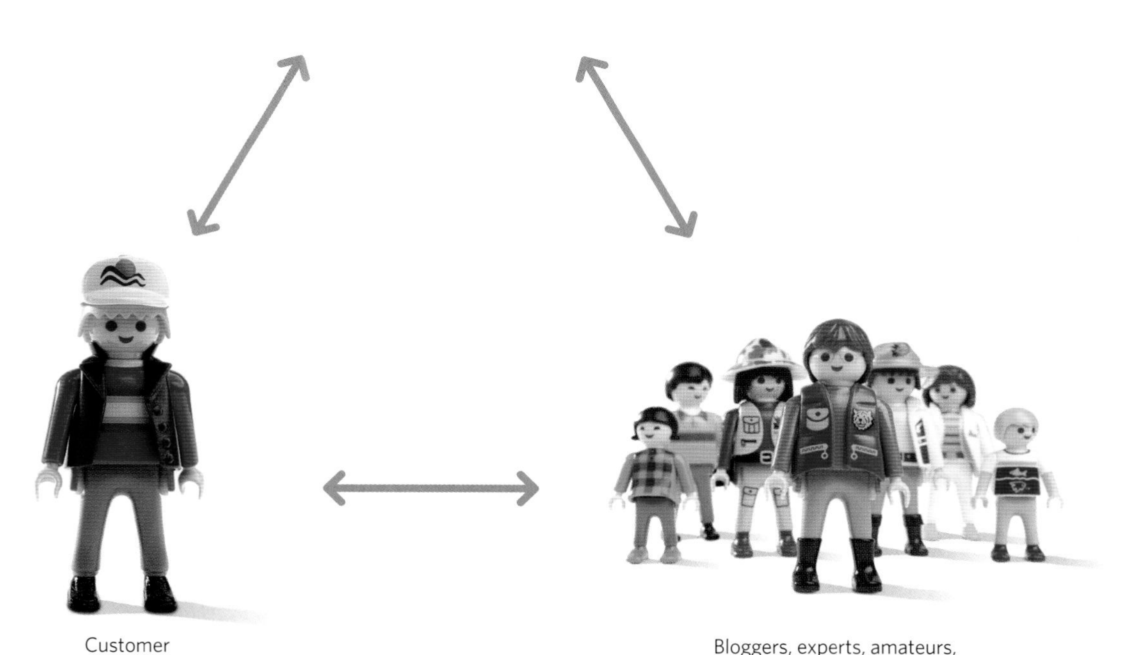

Customer

Bloggers, experts, amateurs, friends, Facebook friends, family, coworkers, online groups, associates, second grade teachers, etc.

Courtesy: People Design
Photos: Jeremy Frechette

58 Ingredient Brands

Logos often look their best when they're set apart, standing alone, all by themselves. Give a mark a nice, clean treatment, and you give a potential customer a clear symbol of the organization you're trying to represent. But in a world where everything from artificial sweeteners to environmental certification programs to software components clamor for graphic recognition, the luxury of a nice, clean treatment doesn't always avail itself to a designer.

Logo alphabet soup is a trend best avoided. As more and more entities team up to produce products and provide services, however, these relationships may need to be expressed in the mark. The same careful considerations that inform the development of individual marks can help you make multiple logos look good together. The Intel Inside program is a primary case study in ingredient branding. The logo was designed to be a secondary image—a logo kicker.

Identify the hierarchy among any group of logos used in concert. Which is dominant? Which is subordinate? It's not a graphic question, it's a communication question—what is intended to be communicated? The graphic identity should express the intent.

Colophon

MONKEY BUSINESS THAT HELPED GET THIS ISSUE OUT: FREEBUBBLES.ORG; "PIMPING OUT" THE COPY CHIEF'S DESK WITH BUBBLE WRAP; SKYDIVING BAREFOOT AND/OR IN A DRESS; GETTING TWO CHILDREN TO MONKEY AROUND WITH A FAKE DINOSAUR; BANANA CREAM PIE; LEARNING THAT A REDUCED-CALORIE DIET MAKES LAB MONKEYS HEALTHIER AND LIVE LONGER; SCARING NEPHEWS JOSH AND TJ STRAIGHT AT ALCATRAZ; PLAYING A GIG IN VICTORIA AT THE V-LOUNGE—A HOTEL, LIQUOR STORE, CHINESE RESTAURANT, BAR, AND STRIP CLUB UNDER ONE ROOF; SHOOTING BB GUNS IN SEBASTOPOL; GETTING SPAT ON WHILE COLLATING WEDDING PROGRAMS; BUYING GRAPE CHEWABLE CHILDREN'S ASPIRIN FROM EVERY WALGREENS IN SAN FRANCISCO; *GOOD NIGHT, GORILLA*; A WORKING VACATION; GERMAN TOURISTS AT TRAVERTINE HOT SPRING FILMING A VIDEO WHILE OTHERS WERE TRYING TO SOAK; THE DESIGN TEAM'S MORNING MEETINGS; FLIP CUP; TREATING *SPACEBALLS* LIKE *THE ROCKY HORROR PICTURE SHOW*; THE ANGRY GORILLA ON "AUTO-TUNE THE NEWS"; SIMIAN MOBILE DISCO.

WIRED IS A REGISTERED TRADEMARK OF ADVANCE MAGAZINE PUBLISHERS INC. COPYRIGHT ©2009 CONDÉ NAST PUBLICATIONS. ALL RIGHTS RESERVED. PRINTED IN THE U.S.A. VOLUME 17, NO. 09. *WIRED* (ISSN 1059-1028) IS PUBLISHED MONTHLY BY CONDÉ NAST PUBLICATIONS, WHICH IS A DIVISION OF ADVANCE MAGAZINE PUBLISHERS INC. EDITORIAL OFFICE: 520 THIRD STREET, STE. 305, SAN FRANCISCO, CA 94107-1815. PRINCIPAL OFFICE: THE CONDÉ NAST BUILDING, 4 TIMES SQUARE, NEW YORK, NY 10036. S. I. NEWHOUSE, JR., CHAIRMAN; CHARLES H. TOWNSEND, PRESIDENT/CEO; JOHN W. BELLANDO, EXECUTIVE VICE PRESIDENT/COO; DEBI CHIRICHELLA SABINO, SENIOR VICE PRESIDENT/CFO; JILL BRIGHT, EXECUTIVE VICE PRESIDENT/HUMAN RESOURCES. PERIODICALS POSTAGE PAID AT NEW YORK, NY, AND AT ADDITIONAL MAILING OFFICES. CANADA POST PUBLICATIONS MAIL AGREEMENT NO. 40644503. CANADIAN GOODS AND TAX REGISTRATION NO. 123242885-RT0001. CANADA ... UNDELIVERABLE CANADIAN ADDRESSES ... MARKHAM, ON L3P 8L4.

UPON DETERMINING THAT POTENTIAL WINNER HAS MET ALL ELIGIBILITY REQUIREMENTS OF THE PROMOTION, INCLUDING WITHOUT LIMITATION THE EXECUTION OF REQUIRED WAIVERS, PUBLICITY AND LIABILITY RELEASES AND DISCLAIMERS, SUCH INDIVIDUAL WILL BE DECLARED THE "WINNER" OF THE PROMOTION.

ALL FEDERAL, STATE AND/OR LOCAL INCOME AND OTHER TAXES, IF ANY, ARE THE WINNER'S SOLE RESPONSIBILITY.

BY ENTERING THE PROMOTION, EACH ENTRANT RELEASES AND DISCHARGES THE SPONSOR, AND ANY OTHER PARTY ASSOCIATED WITH THE DEVELOPMENT OR ADMINISTRATION OF THIS PROMOTION, THEIR PARENT, SUBSIDIARY, AND AFFILIATED ENTITIES, AND EACH OF THEIR RESPECTIVE OFFICERS, DIRECTORS, MEMBERS, SHAREHOLDERS, EMPLOYEES, INDEPENDENT CONTRACTORS, AGENTS, REPRESENTATIVES, SUCCESSORS AND ASSIGNS (COLLECTIVELY, "SPONSOR ENTITIES"), FROM ANY AND ALL LIABILITY WHATSOEVER IN CONNECTION WITH THIS PROMOTION, INCLUDING WITHOUT LIMITATION LEGAL CLAIMS, COSTS, INJURIES, LOSSES OR DAMAGES, DEMANDS OR ACTIONS OF ANY KIND (INCLUDING WITHOUT LIMITATION PERSONAL INJURIES, DEATH, DAMAGE TO, LOSS OR DESTRUCTION OF PROPERTY, RIGHTS OF PUBLI... OR PRIVACY, DEFAMATION, OR PORTRAYAL IN A FALSE LIGH... (COLLECTIVELY, "CLAIMS"). EXCEPT WHERE PROHIBITED: (I) ACCEPTANCE OF A PRIZE CONSTITUTES THE CONSENT OF ANY WINNER, WITHOUT FURTHER COMPENSATION, TO USE THE NAME AND LIKENESS OF SUCH WINNER AND HIS/HER SUBMISSION FOR EDITORIAL, ADVERTISING AN... PUBLICITY PURPOSES BY THE SPONSOR AND/OR OTHE... AUTHORIZED BY THE SPONSOR; (II) ACCEPTANCE OF A ... CONSTITUTES A RELEASE BY ANY WINNER OF THE SP... ENTITIES OF ANY AND ALL CLAIMS IN CONNECTION W... THE ADMINISTRATION OF THIS PROMOTION AND THE ... MISUSE, OR POSSESSION OF HIS/HER SUBMISSION O... PRIZE; (III) ANY POTENTIAL WINNER MAY BE REQUI... TO SIGN AN AFFIDAVIT OF ELIGIBILITY (INCLUDING ... SECURITY NUMBER) AND A LIABILITY/PUBLICITY/... RELEASE. AFFIDAVITS AND RELEASES MUST BE R... WITHIN TEN (10) DAYS FROM THE DATE THAT SP... TRIES TO NOTIFY THE POTENTIAL WINNER... A MINOR UNDER THE JURISDI... PRIZE WILL BE AWAR... GUARDIA...

Brand*

*Powered by Another Brand

Brand powered by other brands: Advertising for automobiles and tech gadgets regularly touts the ingredient brands found inside the products being sold.

Photos: Jeremy Frechette

59 Standards of Hierarchy

Strong programs are often about standardized treatments. Making two or more marks work together in a program often requires rules for maintaining the hierarchy of the relationships. These marks are almost never equal. One mark usually leads, and the others represent ingredient brands or product brands that are subordinate. Once the hierarchy standard has been defined, then determine the program pattern.

Ingredient brands have a right to enforce their program identity standards on the companies that use their ingredients. A well-executed program finds a way for ingredient logos to add to the program identity. Often, the ingredient brands lend credibility, like medals on a scout uniform.

Whether the lead brand is Mac-compatible or as-seen-on-Food Network, the visual vocabulary established by a standardized program treatment clearly implies the business relationship.

Brand hierarchy

Brand partnership

1

The Bookmarked Club builds on the recognizable Target brand, while the Bags identity program stands on its own in contrast with the graphic identity of whatever the airline the company may be servicing.

UNITED

Remote Check-in Services by Bags

1. Bookmarked
Wink
Richard Boynton, Scott Thares

2. Bags
Push
Chris Robb, Mark Unger, Gordon Weller, Forest Young, Randall Morris, Renda Morton, Pedro Gomez, Steven Marshall

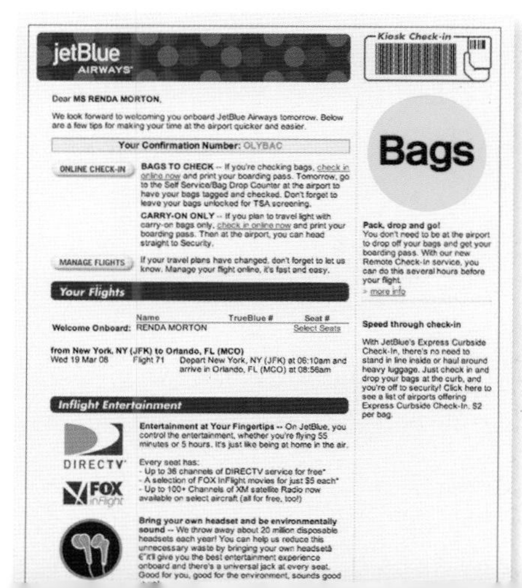

jetBlue AIRWAYS

Kiosk Check-in

Dear **MS RENDA MORTON**,

We look forward to welcoming you onboard JetBlue Airways tomorrow. Below are a few tips for making your time at the airport quicker and easier.

Your Confirmation Number: OLYBAC

ONLINE CHECK-IN

BAGS TO CHECK -- If you're checking bags, check in online now and print your boarding pass. Tomorrow, go to the Self Service/Bag Drop Counter at the airport to have your bags tagged and checked. Don't forget to leave your bags unlocked for TSA screening.

CARRY-ON ONLY -- If you plan to travel light with carry-on bags only, check in online now and print your boarding pass. Then at the airport, you can head straight to Security.

MANAGE FLIGHTS

If your travel plans have changed, don't forget to let us know. Manage your flight online, it's fast and easy.

Your Flights

	Name	TrueBlue #	Seat #
Welcome Onboard:	RENDA MORTON		Select Seats

from New York, NY (JFK) to Orlando, FL (MCO)
Wed 19 Mar 08 Flight 71 Depart New York, NY (JFK) at 06:10am and arrive in Orlando, FL (MCO) at 08:56am

Inflight Entertainment

DIRECTV

FOX inFlight

Entertainment at Your Fingertips -- On JetBlue, you control the entertainment, whether you're flying 55 minutes or 5 hours. It's just like being at home in the air.

Every seat has:
- Up to 36 channels of DIRECTV service for free*
- A selection of FOX InFlight movies for just $5 each*
- Up to 100+ Channels of XM satellite Radio now available on select aircraft (all for free, too!)

Bring your own headset and be environmentally sound -- We throw away about 20 million disposable headsets each year! You can help us reduce this unnecessary waste by bringing your own headsetâ €"it'll give you the best entertainment experience onboard and there's a universal jack at every seat. Good for you, good for the environment, sounds good

Bags

Pack, drop and go!
You don't need to be at the airport to drop off your bags and get your boarding pass. With our new Remote Check-in service, you can do this several hours before your flight.
> more info

Speed through check-in

With JetBlue's Express Curbside Check-In, there's no need to stand in line inside or haul around heavy luggage. Just check in and drop your bags at the curb, and you're off to security! Click here to see a list of airports offering Express Curbside Check-In. $2 per bag.

2

60 Managing Multiple Brands

The question of how multiple brand identities might peacefully coexist only recently became an issue. In the past, you might have seen multiple logos on a NASCAR driver's jumpsuit, but you wouldn't see a jumble of logos on the same magazine advertisement. Today, companies create logos for things that may or may not even warrant their own identity. How committed is Lincoln to Ecoboost technology?

The first choice is whether or not a company needs multiple brands. A good rule of thumb: Don't build another brand until you have to. More brands mean more money.

If an organization establishes multiple, overlapping brands, the question of whether the organization should become a branded house or remain behind the scenes as a house of brands needs to be considered. Very few companies actually have the wherewithal to create a house of brands. Up until it reorganized after emerging from bankruptcy protection, General Motors was widely criticized for maintaining too many brands. Brands are expensive to build and maintain. In general, fewer is better. Ultimately, companies that are deliberate about their brand strategy and stay the course will win out in the end.

BRANDED HOUSE

Too big to fail.

HOUSE OF BRANDS

If you think it's hard
to run a country, try the
United Nations.

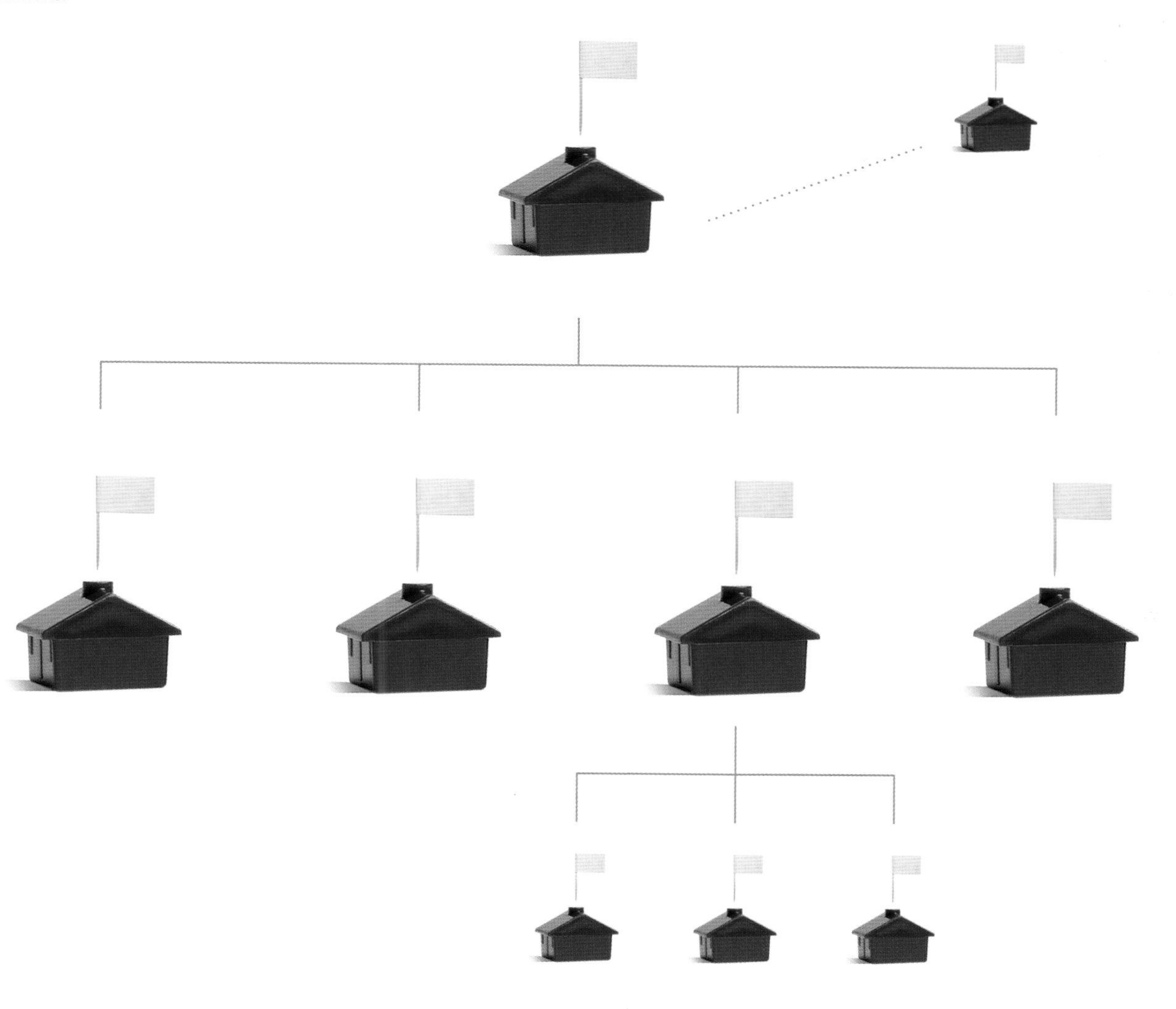

Courtesy: People Design

61 Trademarks

Originality is seldom the explicit client goal of a new graphic identity project, but stretching yourself to develop a graphic identity that doesn't look like anything else may help legally protect the mark in the marketplace.

Just like names and taglines, the law recognizes a company's logo as its intellectual property. Of course, a designer wouldn't intentionally create a logo that looked like an existing mark (especially in the same category or industry). However, so many logos have been developed in the last sixty years that finding common, universally understood shapes or cultural icons that haven't already been used can be difficult.

Beginning your identity projects with research may make it harder to finish the work, but research must be included at some point in your design process. The ready availability of information and logo databases can help you find out whether you are getting close to a violation.

It didn't take long for the People Design team to realize that their Pulse Roller mark looks similar to many marks already in existence—including dtox day spa. From an intellectual property standpoint, however, Pulse Roller is free to use the mark without fear of legal action because none of the companies with similar logos were direct competitors.

10 Tips for Developing a Protectable Graphic Identity

SOURCE
Mary C. Bonnema, Attorney
McGarry Bair PC, Trademark Protection and Litigation
mcgarrybair.com

1. Don't be a copycat!
   Make your identity unique and legally protectable.
2. Don't adopt a descriptive identity.
   For example, *The Books & Mugs Store* is too hard to protect.
3. Don't step on toes.
   Be aware of comparable trademarks or trade dress.
4. Evaluate risk.
   Get a risk-assessment search and legal opinion done on any brand names/taglines/logos/trade dress you plan to use.
5. Protect patentable ideas.
   If your new identity involves a new and unique invention, seek patent counsel as soon as possible.
6. Protect trademarks.
   Register any trademarks associated with your new identity.
7. Protect copyrights.
   Register any copyrights associated with your new identity.
8. Use proper notice markings.
   It may be a bother, but use TM, SM, ®, ©, and "patent pending" for your intellectual property (IP) on the product, packaging, and in marketing and promotions.
9. Manage your IP assets.
   If another company or outside individual helps you with your identity, logos, trade dress, copyrights, etc., make sure their IP rights are assigned/transferred to your company so you can own and enforce those rights.
10. Ask for help.
    When in doubt—and even when not in doubt—seek IP counsel.

1. Pulse Roller
People Design

2. dtox day spa
Special Modern Design
Karen Barranco

3. Mercantile Exchange
TOKY Branding + Design
Eric Thoelke, Travis Brown

4. Morningside Athletic Club
Cue, Inc.
Alan Colvin

1

2

3

4

62 Trade Dress

As logos become more and more ubiquitous—and as competition gets stiffer and stiffer—the need to develop identity programs that help differentiate organizations from their competitors increases in significance.

The first step is creating a mark that's completely yours, but that's only the first step. The next step challenges you to think about how to apply that mark in ways that add up to a unique and protectable program, one that echoes the brand promise and speaks to the intended audience in a way that others have not.

In legal terms, protecting the overall look and feel of an identity program falls under trade dress. The placement of the mark, the color, the shape of product packaging: All of the things that create the overall look and feel of a brand in the marketplace could be a trade dress.

Trade dress is difficult to protect. For some types of trade dress, you need to prove that the consumer really believes that the trade dress is a source indicator for you—that your company is the source of that product or package. For example, the unique curved shape of the Coca-Cola bottle is protected as a trade dress. Only once a company proves that it's package or program has achieved distinctiveness can it be protected as trade dress.

The silhouettes of several Herman Miller products have trade dress protection.

Courtesy: Herman Miller, Inc.

The shape of Coca-Cola bottles is a brand identifier that is almost as important as its logo.

Photos: Jeremy Frechette, Terry Johnston

63 Owning an Aesthetic

Protecting the brand identity in a legal sense becomes even harder than identity programs, but attempting to "own" a meaningful space in the mind of your customer is every marketer's objective. Being cognizant and proactive in projecting and protecting brand identity turf is worth the investment to keep a company sharp and competitors at bay.

Hershey's capitalizes on its recognizable brands for its Times Square presence in New York City.

Hershey's
BIG/Ogilvy
Brian Collins, Edward Chiquitucto, Roman Luba, Weston Bingham

Reese's

HERSHEY'S

HERSHEY'S
MILK CHOCOLATE
NET WT.
1.55 OZ.
(43 g)
Kit Kat
CRISP WAFERS IN CHOCOLATE
Whatchamacallit
York
Get the sensation!
CHOCOLATE COVERED
PEPPERMINT PATTIE
Mounds
Peter Paul
KING SIZE
4 PIECES
Good & Plenty
JOLLY RANCHER
HARD CANDY
CHERRY
HERSHEY'S
SPECIAL DARK
HERSHEY'S
mr. Goodbar
PEANUTS IN MILK C
PayDay
Reese's
NutRageous
MILK CHOCOLATE · PEANUTS · CARAMEL
Cool Mint
ICE BREAKERS
krackel
CRISPED RICE IN MILK CHOCOLATE
Reese's
MILK CHOCOLATE
2 PEANUT BUTTER CUPS
NET WT 1.6 OZ (45 g)
As Always A Low Fat Candy
Twizzlers
STRAWBERRY TWISTS
HEATH
MILK CHOCOLATE ENGLISH TOFFEE BAR
HERSHEY'S
KISSES
MILK CHOCOLATE
Peter Paul
Almond
KING SIZE
4 PIECES
Milk Chocolate
Coconut
JOLLY RANCHER
HARD CANDY
ORIGINAL ASSORTMENT
Cookies'n'Creme
Chocolate cookie bits in white chocolate
DELICIOUS COOKIE RECIPE ON BACK

64 Logo Specs

Once you've arrived at a perfect drawing or configuration for your graphic identity, take the time to write it down. Documenting the origin and development of a graphic identity challenges designers to work out what's been going on in their heads. Quite often, this process also leads to refinements that improve the mark.

Articulating these ideas amounts to more than self-exploration. Documenting a graphic identity this way also allows you to share a record of your decision-making process—and the wisdom behind it. This record can build in room for variation while protecting against compromising the integrity of the mark. It establishes rules, guidelines, dos, and don'ts.

It isn't any arrow; it is *this* arrow. It isn't any serif typeface; it is Bodoni. Anything less adds up to something that is not this graphic identity.

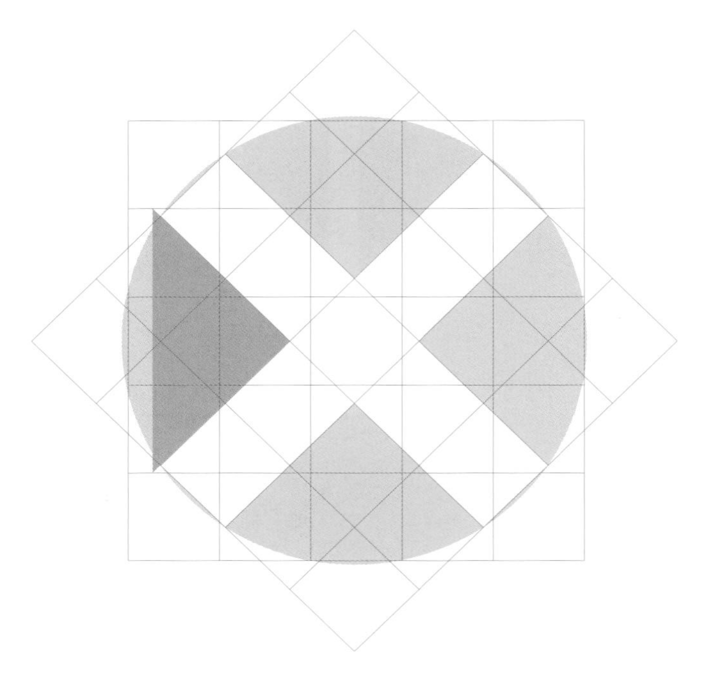

1

2

3

A thorough set of logo specs should cover the precise drawing of a logo, the position of elements, spacing, color, and proximity to other elements. Attention to detail here can add to an overall sense of quality and craft, and set a tone for the overall program.

1. X-Rite
People Design

2. Agility
Siegel+Gale
Sven Seger, Marcus Bartlett, Monica Chai, Inesa Figueroa, Holmfridur Hardardottir

3. Companion Baking
designlab, inc.
Scott Gericke, Patrick Davis Partners, Douglas Allebach

4. The Florida State University
Siegel+Gale
Sven Seger, Anne Swan, Johnny Lim, Austyn Stevens, Hayley Berlent

5. Indiana University
samatamason
Jack Jacobi, Kevin Krueger, Dave Mason, Jeremy Smith

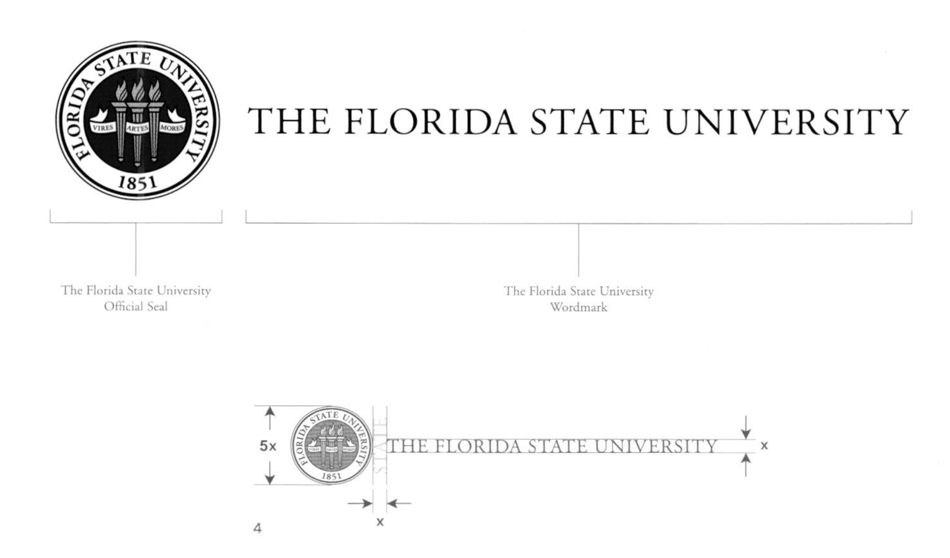

4

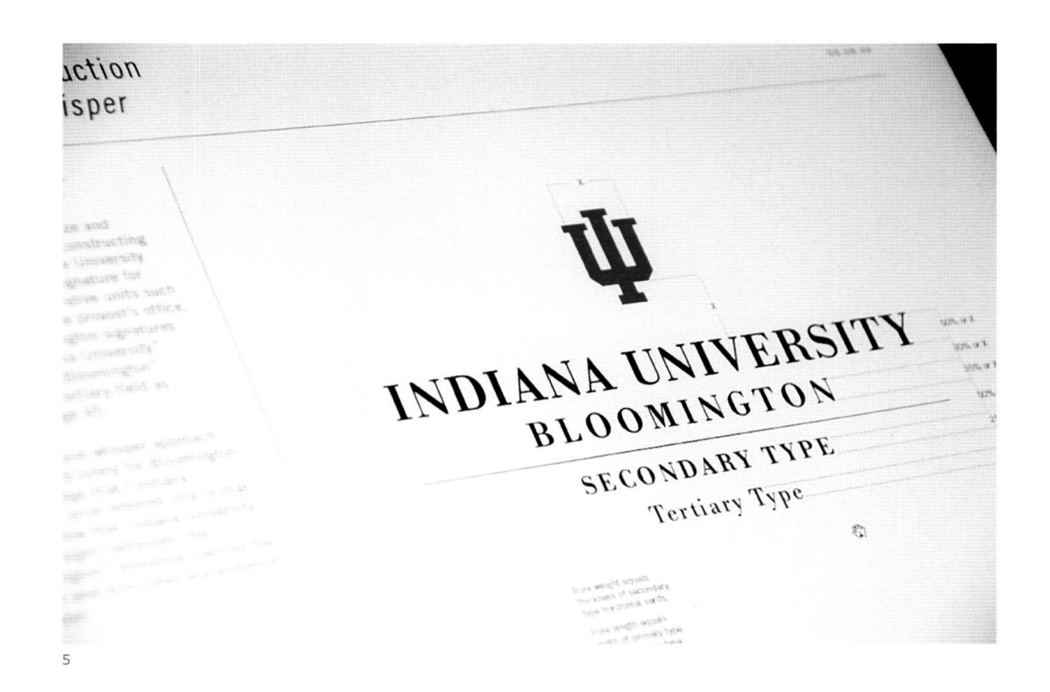

5

65 Application Rules

Creating and following application rules are essential for ensuring program consistency. And creating application specifications allows for it to be done by more than one person.

Large firms work with many business and creative partners as well as vendors and suppliers who make decisions on a daily basis about how a mark is applied—and they probably shouldn't. Nonetheless, if identity specs are written clearly and designed well, and if they are presented positively and enthusiastically, most partners will see them as a burden lifted rather than a new one added.

Identity program specs might address scale, position, color, proximity, and number:

Scale—How large or small is the mark relative to the overall size of a sign, etc.?

Position—What is the mark's position relative to other elements? How close can it be to the edge of a business card? How must it align with other things?

Color—Is the mark always the same color on the same background color?

Proximity—What other typographic or visual elements accompany the mark?

Number—How many marks appear on the side of a building? Forty or one?

Program specs should define the rules, but with enough latitude for experimentation.

Careful documentation of program rules and guidelines serves as a record of decisions made, helping to police consistency and quality.

Hellomoto
50,000feet

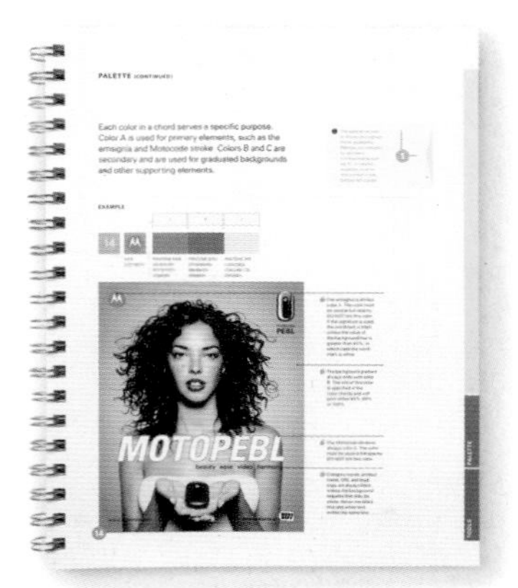

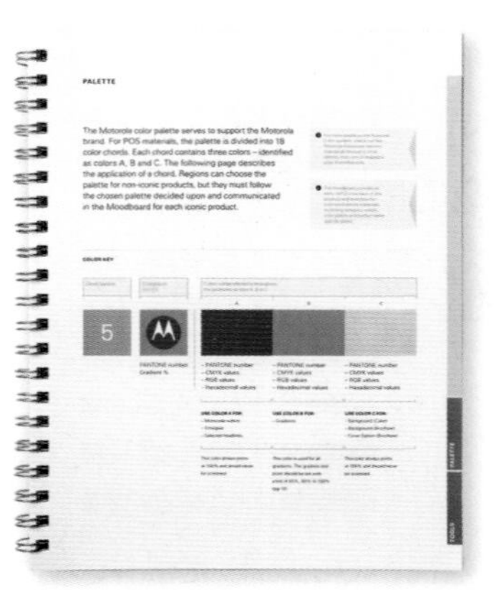

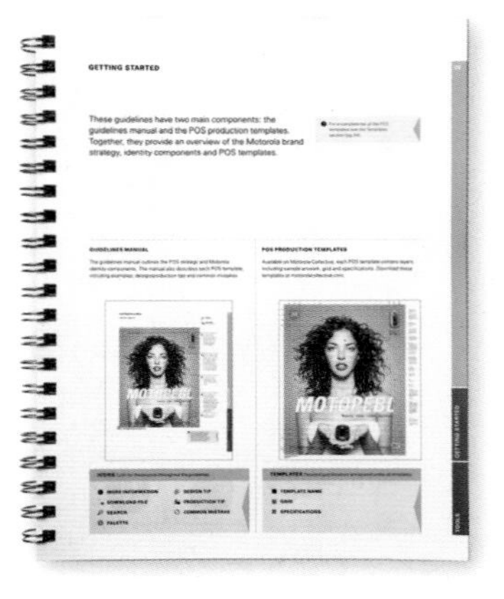

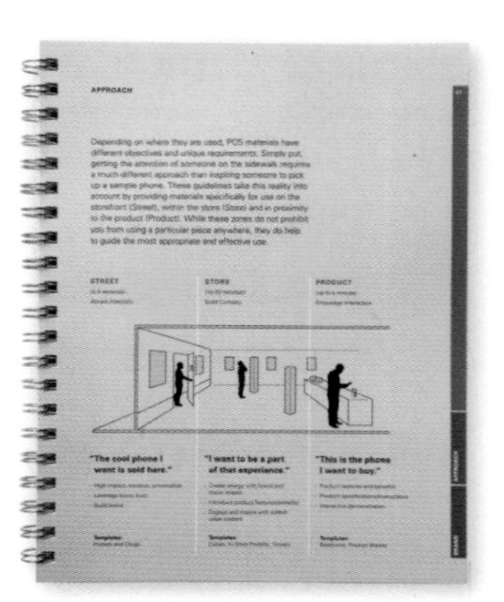

Global Color Study

Color Choice Categories

Indigenous Architecture

Packaged Goods

Clothing

Advertising

Color Distribution Across All Regions

Image Selection All Regions

Colors Plotted On Color Wheel

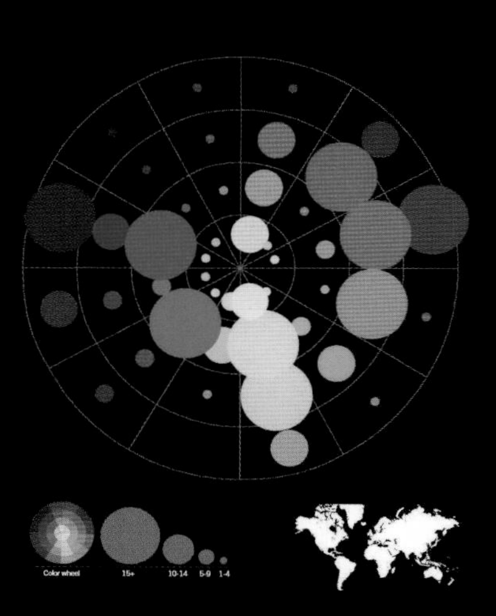

New Color Palette

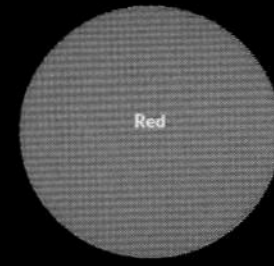

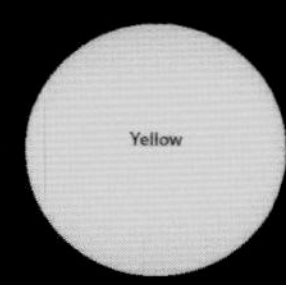

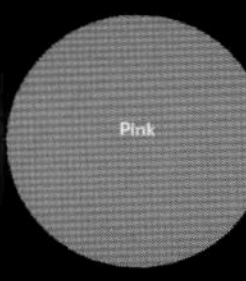

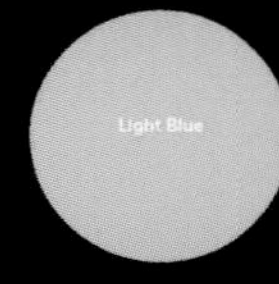

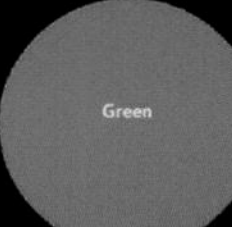

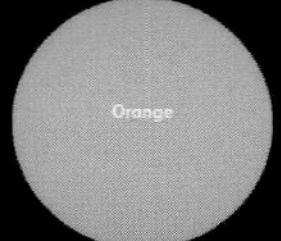

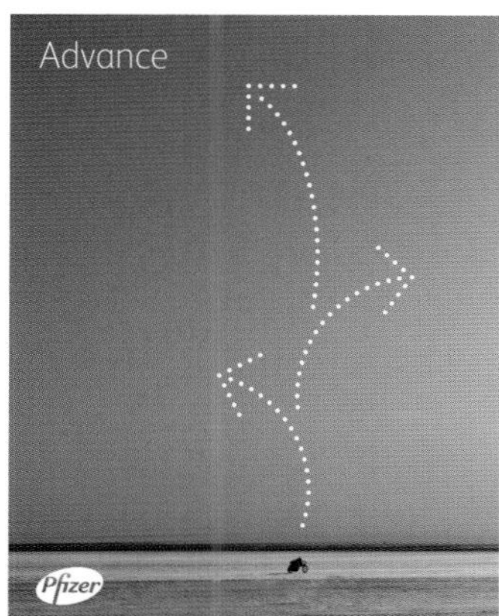

Pfizer
Siegel+Gale
Howard Belk, Sven Seger, Young Kim, Johnny Lim, Monica Chai, Quae Luong, David McCanless

66 Brand Bibles

When some people think "bible," they think rulebook. Others think of it as a book of inspiration. Most people who read it tend to find a little of both.

Imagine these two modes—rules and inspiration—separated into two different books. That's what most organizations do when they want to document their brand. Brand guidelines contain the dos and don'ts of a brand. Brand bibles capture its spirit and promise.

Brand bibles trace their roots back to the elaborate annual reports companies began producing in the 1970s. At that time, well-known designers helped companies seize an opportunity presented by their SEC-mandated annual financial reports. If done well, these documents could communicate something to stockholders beyond earnings. Designers recreated the front-door experience for investors, seeking buy-in through corporate cheerleading.

Years later, as companies moved their financials online, a new generation of designers encouraged companies to continue publishing the promotional part of their annual reports for internal use. The brand bible was born. Since companies no longer refresh their brands in annually produced reports, these brand bibles became more precious.

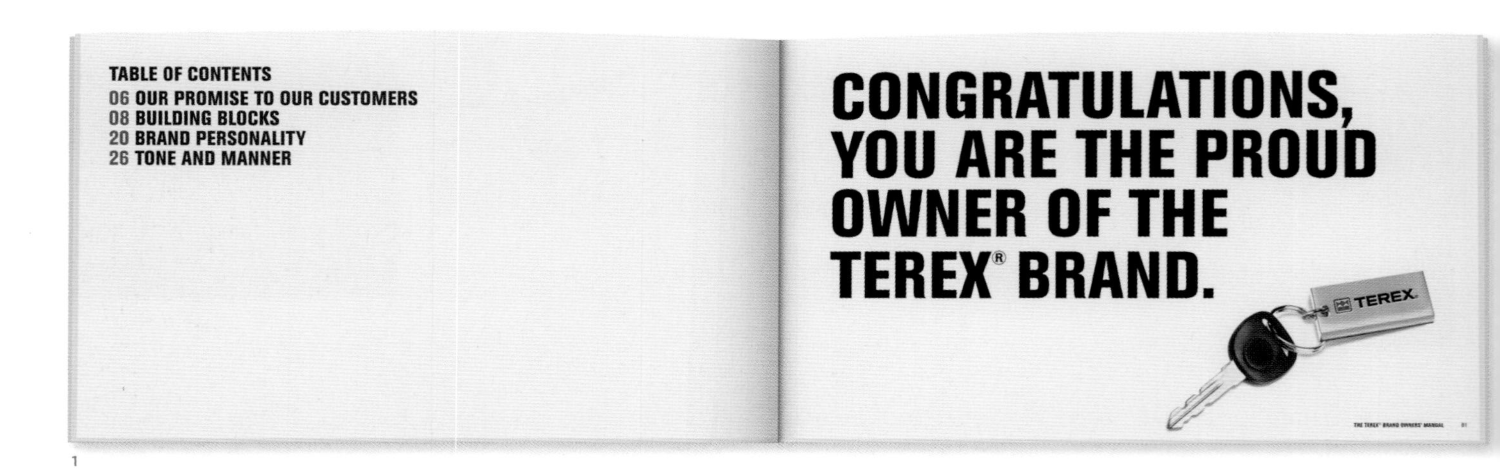

1

These brand bibles enlist bold claims and metaphorical imagery to move primarily internal audiences to realize the potential of their brands.

1. Terex
Siegel+Gale
Matt Huss, Sven Seger, Doug Sellers, Johnny Lim, Luma Eldin, Alex Kroll

2. Emblem Health
Siegel+Gale
Jenifer Books, Sven Seger, Young Kim, Michelle Matthews, Luma Eldin, Frank Oswald

3. Service Source
C2
Erik Cox, Greg Galle, John Bielenberg

2

Get your Emblem on.

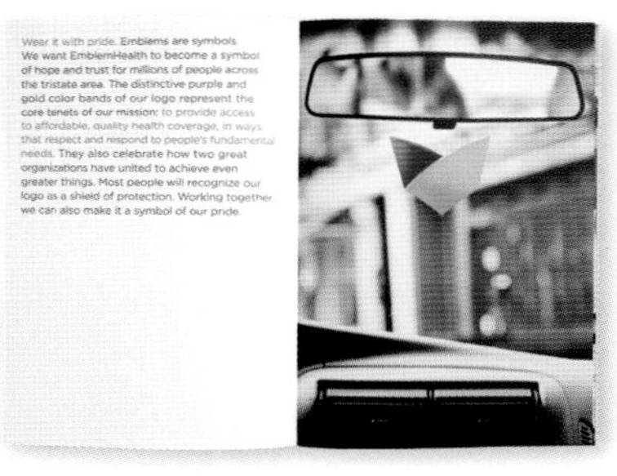

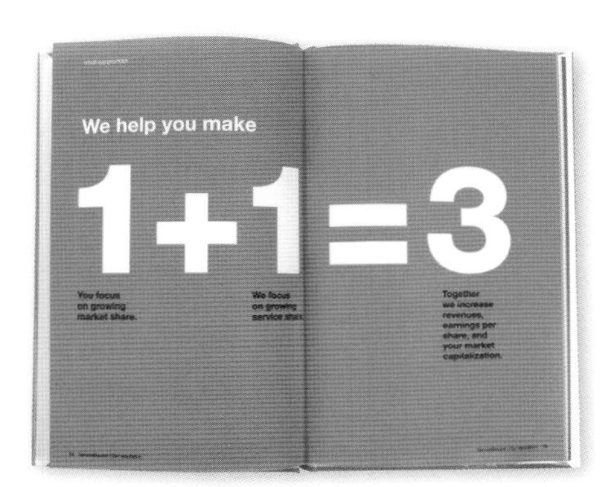

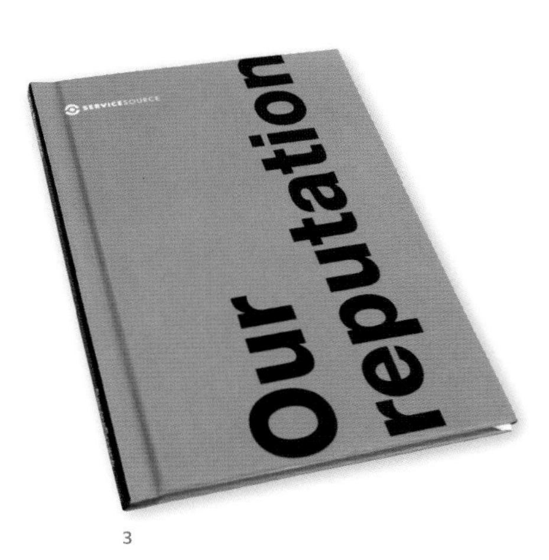

3

67 Logos Lifecycles

Times change. People change. And the identities of some organizations—although not all—change right along with them.

Why is it that some logos seem to age well while others do not? AT&T, UPS, and Burger King have all updated their graphic identities in recent years, while Volkswagen, CBS, and the Olympic Games have not.

Certain graphic elements age better than others. Companies pin the fate of their illustrative logos on the longevity of the particular drawing style they chose. Typefaces are increasingly susceptible to looking dated, which may account for some degree of graphic identity reinvention. Like hairstyles and clothing, certain graphic embellishments go out of fashion as quickly as they come into favor.

Simple, bold, easily identifiable marks possess a timeless quality. What plausible reason could Volkswagen give for changing its classic logo? The company's current mark could easily outlive the updated marks of AT&T and UPS. If it does, which will build the most equity in the mind of customers over time?

When developing a graphic identity, consider the lifecycle of the mark. Don't let it paralyze decision making or push you toward solutions that may prove to be too conservative, but ask yourself: Is this a mark the client could live with for the next fifty years?

Before

After

1

Before

After

2

Evolving a graphic identity can involve a complete redo, or minor refinements to help keep brands feeling current.

1. X-Rite
People Design

2. Meredith Identity
Lippincott
Connie Birdsall, Jenifer Lecker, Shelby Brea

3. Smokey Bones
Push
Chris Robb, Mark Unger, Kevin Taylor, Gordon Weller, Kevin Harre

4. ICFJ
Siegel+Gale
Sven Seger, Young Kim, Daniella Spinat

5. Pfizer
Siegel+Gale
Howard Belk, Sven Seger, Young Kim, Johnny Lim, Monica Chai, Quae Luong, David McCanless

6. Rebranding of CEC Bank
Brandient
Cristian "Kit" Paul, Alin Tamansan, Eugen Erhan, Bogdan Dumitrache, Cristian Petre, Iancu Barbarasa

Before

After

SMOKEY
BONES
Bar & Fire Grill

3

Before

International Center
for Journalists

After

International Center
for Journalists

4

Before

After

5

Before

After

6

68 Planning for Change

Commitment to an identity program over a defined period of time makes sense, though identity programs are made for reinvention. Organizations often coordinate program changes with scheduled events: a product launch, a trade show, an advertising campaign. Built-in plans to evolve allow organizations to anticipate the next event with less internal heartburn over the changes.

Every opportunity to keep the identity program fresh and relevant also represents an opportunity to react to changing market conditions and shifting customer needs. Programs provide the necessary space for an identity to evolve, but change just for the sake of change doesn't necessarily contribute to a better brand experience—just a different one. Designing dynamic programs requires knowing what should remain constant.

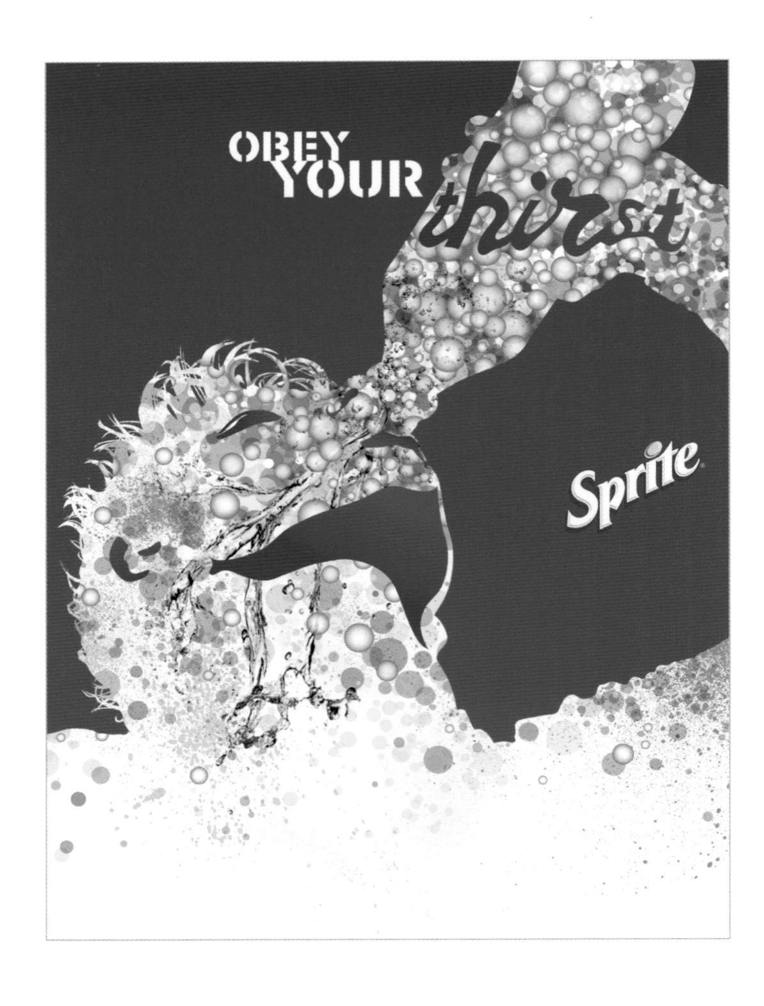

The future ain't what it used to be: Sprite continues to appeal to a youthful demographic with exciting graphics that challenge and inspire.

Sprite
BIG/Ogilvy
Brian Collins, Maja Blazejewska, Satian Pengsathapon, Jason Ring, Iwona Waluk, Weston Bingham

FRESH
obey
your
thirst
Sprite

Sprite
obey
your
thirst
FRESH
Sprite

OBEY YOUR
THIRST
Sprite

OBEY YOUR
THIRST
Sprite

THIRST
OBEY YOUR
THIRST
Sprite

69 Change Strategy

Some markets rely on a sense of stability and consistency. Others thrive on change. You might not expect a law firm or bank to change on a whim, but media companies or other organizations more closely tied to pop culture thrive on change. In the race for brand differentiation, however, the rules are loosening. Next-generation law firms are embracing the new, and bank brands once built on stability are eager to redefine themselves.

Brand identities reflect and evolve with customer needs. Foundational brand attributes form the character of an organization. These do not change; a sense of reliability and continuity depend on that. The evolution of a brand identity is usually the translation of baseline attributes for current conditions. Change is inevitable, but the rate of change for a brand needs to be a strategic choice.

The long-standing Kleenex brand has evolved with its customers from the 1920s to present.

Courtesy: Kimberly-Clark Worldwide, Inc.

KLEENEX
TISSUES
KLEENEX
TISSUES
KLEENEX
Softest and Strongest
KLEENEX

KLEENEX
TISSUES
KLEENEX TISSUES
TEAR OUT

Kleenex
Boutique tissues
KLEENEX BOUTIQUE
TISSUES

Kleenex
Softique

70 Dueling Logos

Fifty years ago, when discussions about graphic design found their way into corporate boardrooms, the idea of creating a unique, graphic representation of a company and what it stands for was new. Today's consumers face a tidal wave of brands, with thousands of logos washing over us every day.

The competition for good logos is steep. Not all logos are good. In fact, many of them aren't. But the sheer number of them makes it harder than ever to stand out. Thankfully, far less competition exists within any one industry or segment. A quick survey of all the logos in an industry might reveal that the majority of logos are blue and blocky. If you're looking to upgrade a graphic identity for a company in this industry, do something different and better that will be uniquely appealing to your audience. It sounds obvious, but too often firms follow the competition, rather than their customers.

Sometimes a graphic identity can stand out on quality alone. A clear, easily readable typeface will often endure beyond a fad font. A good mark can become the foundation for communicating your competitive position.

1

When different brands turn to the same aesthetic elements as the competition did for their graphic identity, being different is a way to stand out. Which coffee brand do you want to buy?

2

3

1. Rocamojo
Evenson Design Group
Stan Evenson, Kera Scott

2. Joe Coffee
Square One Design
Mike Gorman, Karin Lannon

3. Te Aro
Akendi
Ian Chalmers, Athena Herrmann, Rosie Pech

71 Programs That Stand Out

In a world of too many logos, identity programs represent a new horizon for brand development. Even if an organization's logo and all of its competitors' logos look alike—some would say "especially" if this is the case—program designers can pursue widely different applications.

It's important for identity programs to be clearly differentiated not only from competitors, but also from any other experiences. Customers will experience the brand through this type of differentiation. The challenge lies in remaining committed to addressing as many customer touchpoints as possible in the program.

1

All Seasons Wild Bird Store program materials outdo many grocers and health food stores in creating a delectable package. A fashion collection is a study in program reinvention, and the Madame Demode brochure on the opposite page is no exception. Its minimalist graphic approach helps Vanja Solin's photography—and the clothes—stand out.

1. All Season's Wild Bird Store
Imagehaus
Jay Miller

2. Madame Demode
Bunch

madame
demode
able to disable
madame
demode
able to disable
DRESS BACK TO FRONT — W
ELASTIC JACKET

72 Competitive Landscape

A lot of brand positioning work relates to an organization's competition—a brand might be positioned this way, but compared to what? A brand identity is built in part on a competitive position.

Being cognizant of the competition and its positioning is just doing your homework. An ownable brand position doesn't need to be the polar opposite of the competition, but it needs to be distinctive. Even fast followers have unique value propositions and identities—often addressing the competition head on. Avis' "We Try Harder" tagline put a positive spin on the company's status as the second-largest car rental company in the U.S. behind Hertz.

More often than not, competition comes from other alternatives—not necessarily from other companies. Instead of buying apples from your fruit stand, potential customers may save their money and go without apples altogether, or they may buy ice cream instead. How would a good brand manager win them back and make apple eaters out of them again?

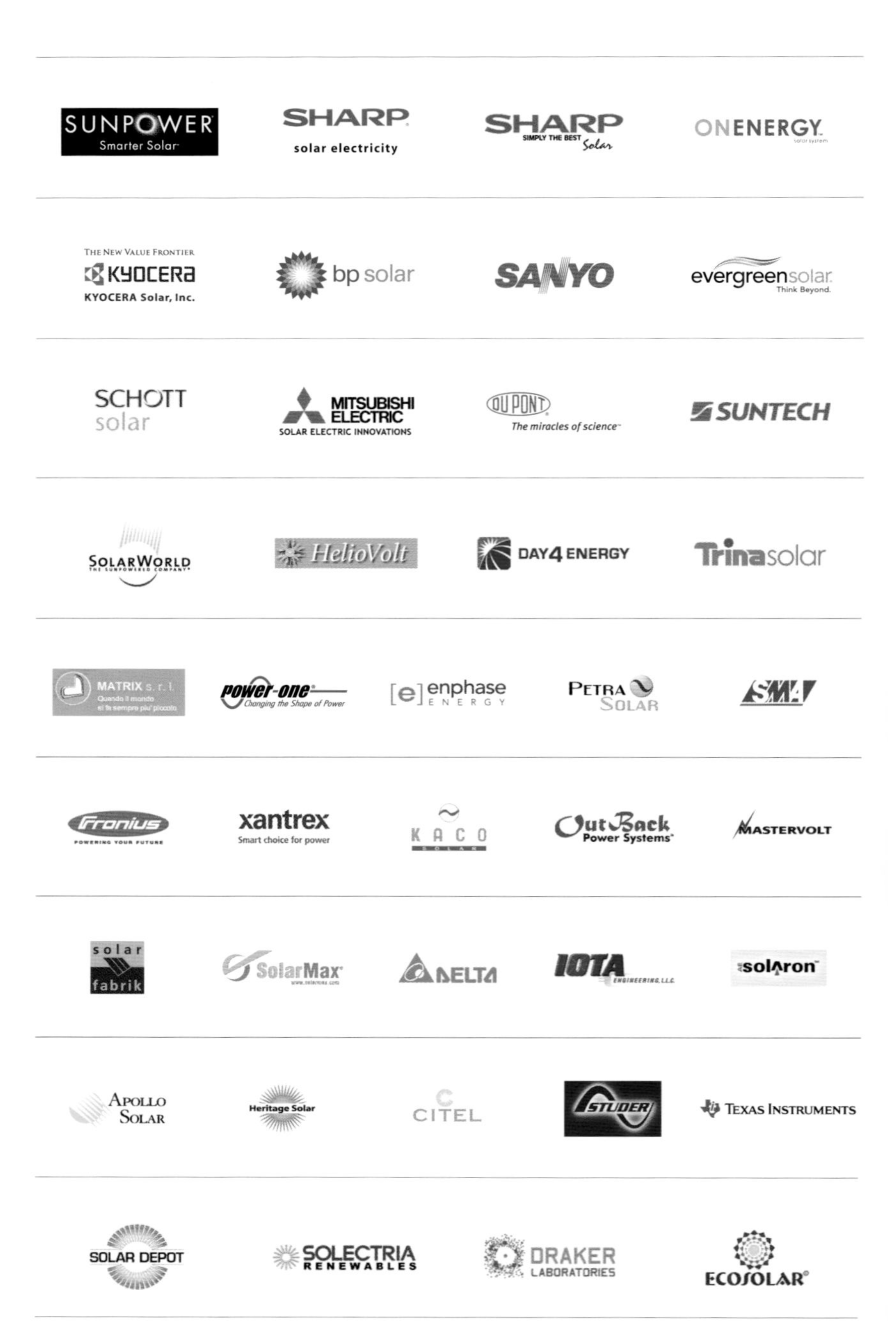

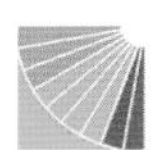

Do your homework. Be aware of what the competition is doing, but to the extent possible, fix your focus on meeting customer needs.

National Semiconductor
SolarMagic Competitive Research
Gee + Chung Design
Earl Gee

73 Timelessness

During the first decades of the twentieth century, graphic identity was a novel idea. As the appetite for logos has increased, the marketplace has grown more crowded. Today, with more marks than ever vying for attention, freshness can be one way to slice through the noise. But freshness is different than originality.

When high-profile companies rebrand themselves with a new logo and a new attitude, sometimes the decisions are wise. Often, they are not. Facelifts don't create an original face; they just make the same old one look a little fresher.

When AT&T hired Saul Bass to design the mark that would become their famous Bell System logo in 1969, the company remained committed to the mark until its break-up in 1983. The freshness may have worn off, but over its fourteen-year run, Bass's Bell Telephone logo enjoyed a 93 percent recognition rate in the U.S.

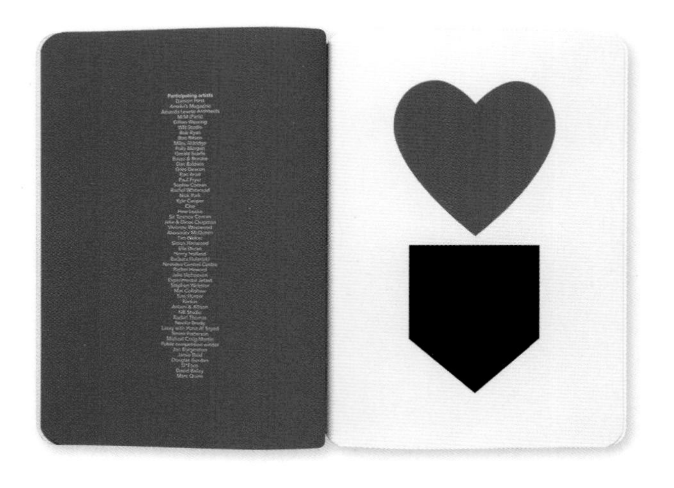

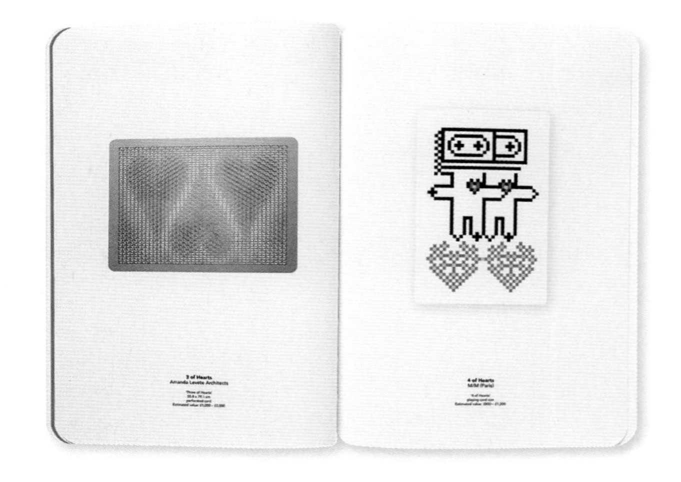

Black and red are timeless colors for graphic identities—and very appropriate for House of Cards. The bold, confident palette helps visualize the name graphically even apart from the mark itself.

House of Cards
Pentagram
Domenic Lippa

Some of the most effective graphic identities rely more on a sense of enduring quality than on originality per se. Cuisipro employs a classic modern style that looks like it could have been designed in 1960—and we mean that as a compliment.

Cuisipro
Hahn Smith Design
Nigel Smith, Alison Hahn

74 Taking Chances

In the crazy picture-in-a-box world we live in, the chance of doing something graphically that has never been done before has slimmed. The real opportunity for originality opens up when designers take a chance and try something different with a logo in application. Two companies might have pretty similar logos, but express a wildly different aesthetic sensibility when they're applied.

Companies often miss the opportunities presented by identity programs. That's because doing something truly original with an identity program takes guts. Part of the reason the Nike logo succeeded was that it was an original shape, but the company also had the guts to do something different with it. They downplayed or completely removed the company name. That idea isn't going to make it past too many clients, but not only did Nike have the guts to pursue it, they created a cultural icon by doing so.

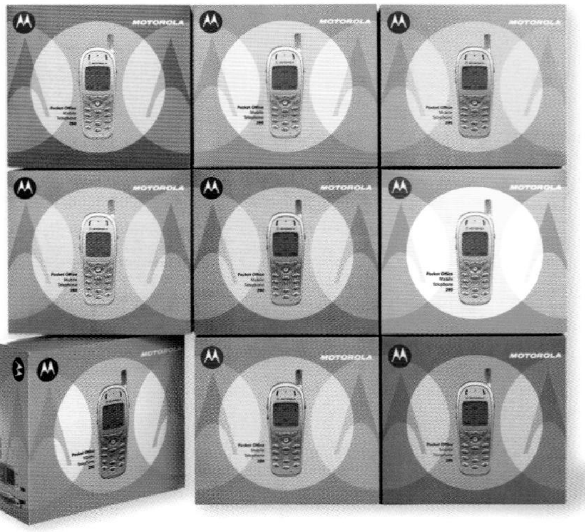

Motorola
BIG/Ogilvy
Brian Collins, Maja Blazejewska, Stella Bugbee, Edward Chiquitucto, Alan Dye, Jason Ring, Thomas Vasquez, Michael Kaye

This Motorola program strikes a balance between the familiar and the new.

75 The Human Element

Some of today's most successful brands capitalize on human emotion. The organizations behind these brands focus not only on achieving business goals but also on meeting human needs.

Competitors might be able to mimic Nike or Apple aesthetically, but what makes these companies true originals isn't the fact that they have beautiful graphic identities and execute them as part of disciplined programs. In both cases, these companies also have built brands that dial into primary human needs. Original thinking developed a brand identity for each company that goes well beyond the products they make.

Originality inspires designers. We like to think that it inspires companies, too.

1

Expressing a a brand's humanity thorough a sense of playfulness (Fujiya, Levi's Kids) or even a sense of craft (Ten) can help a brand identity find an original approach.

1. Fujiya
Wink
Scott Thares, Richard Boynton

2. Levi's Kids
Checkland Kindleysides

3. Ten
Bunch
Bunch, OmegaTheKid!Phoenix and Ivo Sousa, Vanja Solin of Process 15

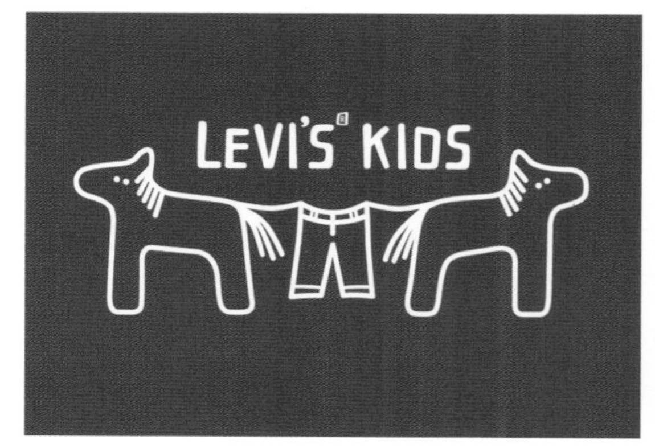

2

FUJI YA
WASABI. UNDERESTIMATE AT YOUR PERIL.
600 WEST LAKE STREET MINNEAPOLIS 612.871.4055

MAGURO (TUNA). SERVED FRESH, VERY FRESH.
FUJI YA
600 WEST LAKE STREET MINNEAPOLIS 612.871.4055

1

T
U

2.
IF
YOU
HAVE
A

3. Some people are

toxic

3

76 Logos with a Sense of Humor

As with art, literature, and life, some of the most memorable work done in the area of graphic identity gives people a reason to smile. While comical logos can easily go too far—after all, you don't want the organization to be perceived as a joke—a clever, witty graphic identity can rise above the rest.

Look into the all-seeing CBS "eye" for an example. One of the major broadcast television networks in the United States, CBS easily could have based its service mark on a more literal image of a TV set or TV camera. Instead, with a wink (pun definitely intended) the network chose to provide a subtle editorial statement on the emergence of the then new media. It may seem obvious today, but it was much less so when William Golden developed the original "eye" in 1951. It remains as clever and relevant today as it was then.

1

2

3

4

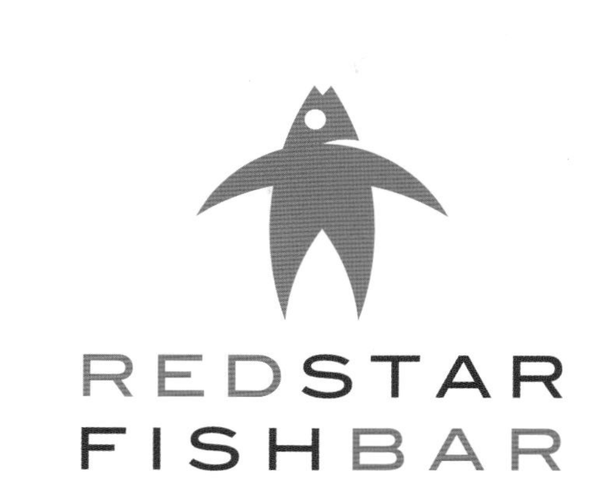

5

6

7

8

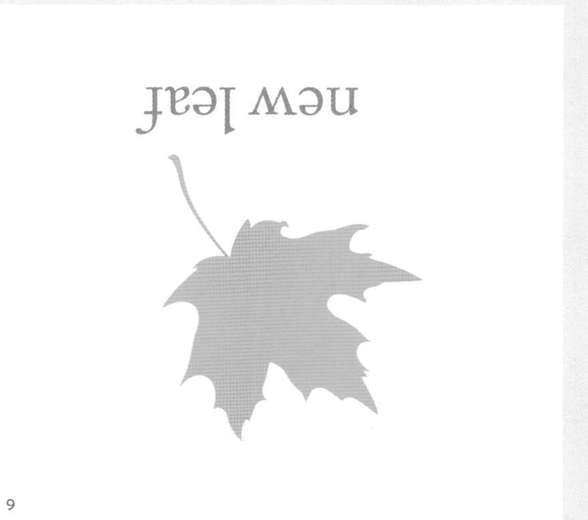

9

Playful marks and clever taglines make us smile.

1. ifpetscouldtype.com
Liska + Associates
Steve Liska, Kim Fry, Katie Schweitzer

2. Yummy Ice Cream
Joao Ricardo Machado

3. Rainbow Cinemas
Joshua Best

4. Little Neuro Tree
Design Nation Pte Ltd.
Joelle Yeo, Jacqueline Neo

5. Red Star Fish Bar
Idea 21 Design
Tom Berno, Jeff Davis

6. Nerdcore Logo
Hexanine
Jason Adam

7. Bellyfeel
G-MAN

8. Buck 'n' Jims
Capsule
Brian Adducci

9. New Leaf Theatre
50,000feet

77 Fun with Programs

Even if your graphic identity has good reason not to attempt to be funny, there may be plenty of room for wit in the program design. Programs are all about context. Given the right time and place, humor can be a strong ally.

The degree of humor in a program can vary depending on the campaign, the timeframe, or the type of media being employed. A witty headline, image, or movie functions like an icebreaker at a meeting. It can loosen things up, prepping the audience for a more serious engagement. Programs often have the luxury of being transitory, so they can employ humor without cracking the bedrock of the brand standards.

1. High Glitz
Liska + Associates
Steve Liska, Kim Fry, Liz Johnson

2. Papane
Brandient
Bogdan Dumitrache, Cristian Petre, Delia Zahareanu

3. The Office of John Cheese
Block Branding
Mark Braddock, Isabel Kruger, Jennifer Berney

1

2

Injecting some wittiness into program applications can be cute, clever, humanizing, and memorable.

"When the crap hits the fan, the only way to stay clean is to be out of the room."

A discussion with the legendary productioneer John Cheese.

The first in a series of three excerpts taken from the original article written by Marshall Miller. Previously published in the American edition of *The Gentleman Magazine*.

Sunlight filtered through the blinds of the city's most private of private clubs. The Cigar Room's thick smoke was elegantly illuminated as I waited to be granted my audience with the enigmatic John Cheese.

"He won't be long," I was assured by one of his many mini-skirted personal assistants.

John Cheese, as you are no doubt aware, is a legend in the digital production industry. The word 'legend' is used far too lightly nowadays, but in the case of Mr. Cheese, the moniker has never been applied more fittingly.

In the late-afternoon's half-glow I found myself contemplating how one who has spent so much of his life avoiding the glare of fame's spotlight becomes so famous. We are all intimately familiar with the great man's work—his creations in screen-based media are the *Mona Lisas* of the digital age—yet we know so little about the man himself.

It was approaching 4:00 PM when yet another blonde assistant entered to inform me that she had received word from the man himself that he was indeed only minutes away. She reported that he was extremely sorry for having kept me waiting.

I learn later that he was 'detained' in a lunch with the French Ambassador who had insisted that Mr. Cheese regail him with stories of Mr. Cheese's service in the Foreign Legion. Rumour has it the lunch ended in the signing of a contract worth in the high seven-figures.

If my sources are correct, Mr. Cheese will be spending considerable time in France over the coming years.

Meanwhile, back at the club, I ordered another Tom Collins and waited.

The next time the Cigar Room's mahogany doors swung open Mr. Cheese was striding intently through them towards me with his hand raised in preparation to dock with mine.

I stood there, momentarily undecided as to what reaction would be appropriate in such a situation. His handshake was firm, yet friendly. It was the handshake of a man who knew how to get what he wanted—a man who never had the need to yell.

This is a man who, for almost two decades, has taken impish delight in stepping on the toes of the industry's traditionalists. He is a maverick and charmer—the type of man every eight year-old boy hopes they will grow up to be.

Over the following two hours, through the smoke of at least a half-dozen Monte Christos, Mr. Cheese shared pearl after perfect pearl of wisdom with me. As hard as it is for a journalist of my standing to admit, it was near impossible for me to keep any degree of subjectivity as he turned the charm up to 'ten' and roasted me, slowly.

As the founder of the Office of John Cheese, Mr. Cheese stalks the concrete canyons of the city casting a shadow that is impressive even for a man of his substantial stature.

I had decided ahead of time that I would start at the beginning. I enquired as to how he had first entered the industry. But from the get-go it was clear that this was a man who likes to set the agenda. He is not one to march to the beat of anyone else's drum.

"Can I be frank?" he counters, "The past is of very little interest to me. We all tend to get into the game for the same couple of reasons—the girls, the money, the power—but these are just short-term distractions. There are few who really have the brains to go to the next level. And I am one of the few."

THE OFFICE OF JOHN CHEESE
DIGITAL PRODUCTION SERVICES
JOHNCHEESE.COM.AU

"Account Managers are credit cards with legs. And I've always been a legs guy."

A discussion with the legendary productioneer John Cheese.

The second in a series of three excerpts taken from the original article written by Marshall Miller. Previously published in the American edition of *The Gentleman Magazine*.

"Really, who cares what I did yesterday?" John Cheese continues, "I certainly don't. What is interesting to me is what I am going to do tomorrow."

And in that one sentence Mr. Cheese summed up the difference between him and the conga-line of pretenders to his throne. "Tomorrow is why I get out of bed in the morning."

He took a drag on his cigar as a way of emphasis followed by a long sip from a snifter that had miraculously appeared on the stand by his chair.

"Look, I've seen it all before. And most of it thrice. Those who lack my street smarts would have you believe I have survived on luck alone.

"That says more about them than it does about me. The reality is that it has been a combination of my nous and my iron *huevos* that have kept me out of trouble. And if you stay out of trouble, you are ninety per cent there."

Despite this self-assurance, Mr. Cheese is the first to admit that it has not always been smooth sailing on his way to the top.

Several years ago his marriage to Hungarian model Boglárka Zoltán Czinkóczi ended in a divorce settlement, the details of which have never been made public.

When pressed on the topic of women Mr. Cheese became quite guarded.

"Let me say just this on the topic: I have never been particularly good at keeping my professional and my private lives separate," he said with a certain melancholy creeping into his tone, "We all have our peccadillos, and this has been mine."

Mr. Cheese possesses at least two qualities rarely seen in busy and successful men. His associates maintain that he is overconscientious about almost everything and that he goes to great lengths to avoid hurting people's feelings.

"I run one of the world's most successful business empires. I have achieved this by surrounding myself with the best and the brightest people. And some of these individuals happen to be particularly good-looking.

"This is a combination that I have found difficult to resist at times.

"If I have learnt anything from these indiscretions it is that if you spend your time chasing tail, eventually you will end up with sh** on your nose," and with that it was clear that Mr. Cheese had said all he had to say on the matter.

Friends of Mr. Cheese are quick to point out that his caring attitude extends far beyond those humans with which he shares his professional and private lifes.

An old friend of Mr. Cheese's recalled to me how, once, on a business trip in Miami, Mr. Cheese came across 14 cats cooped up in an old monkey cage on the grounds of a swank hotel. Mr. Cheese instantly made arrangements to have them cared for on his 1,200-acre Thoroughbred fish farm.

"In this game everyone wants a piece of you. To survive you have to be cunning and tough, but nowhere does it say you can't do that with style and class," said Mr. Cheese.

And I believed him. It is hard not to when he is sitting opposite me wearing a $10,000 suit and sipping $200 nips.

John Cheese is a man who can straddle many worlds. He is a man who defies categorisation, for as soon as you think you have him worked out, he shifts shape again.

No wonder the ladies like him.

THE OFFICE OF JOHN CHEESE
DIGITAL PRODUCTION SERVICES
JOHNCHEESE.COM.AU

3

78 Funny Brands

A key driver guiding whether or not to inject some humor into a graphic identity is whether or not the brand identity has a sense of humor. Not all organizations should try to pull off a wacky logo. On the other hand, a little humor may be a way to help a brand stand out.

Like people, brands with a sense of humor are nice to be around. In addition to providing simple entertainment, wit can have a humanizing effect on a brand. It can show an audience that there are real people behind the corporation.

With social media moving organizations and their brands into personal spaces, revealing the human side of a brand has never been more important. Wit can provide a pathway for deeper, more personal, lasting relationships between companies and their customers.

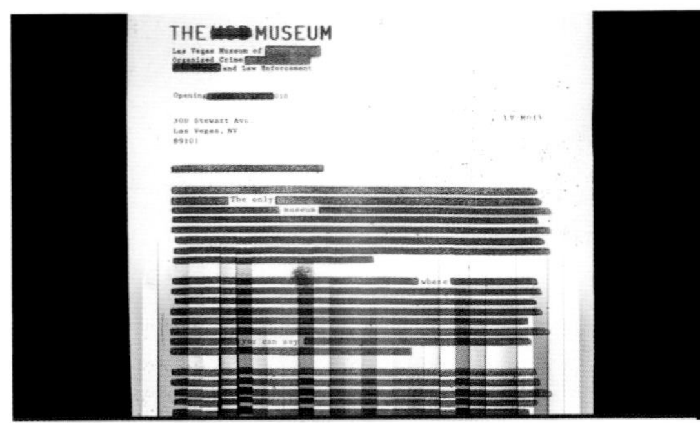

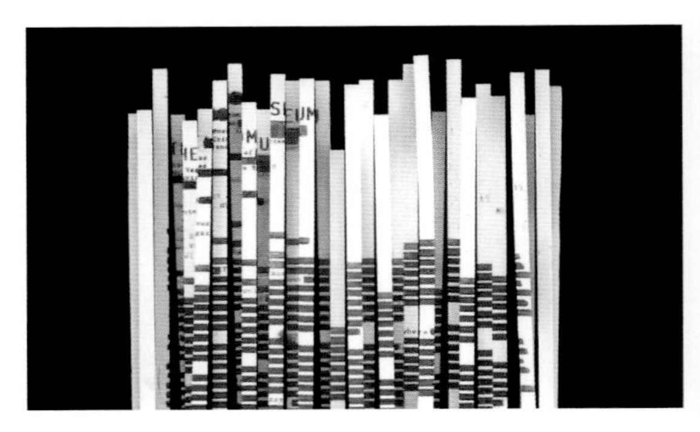

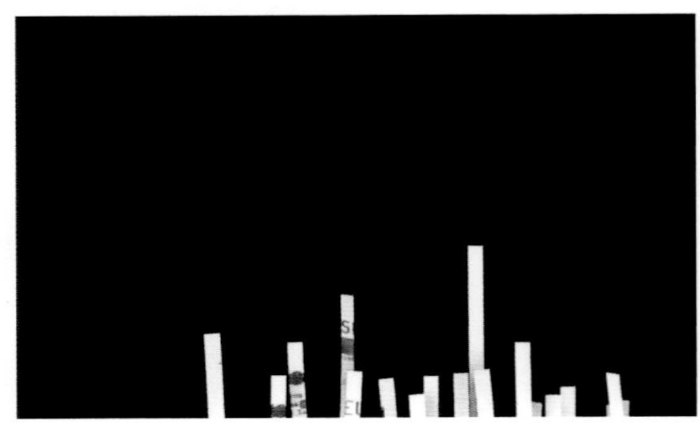

The Mob Museum
Wall-to-Wall Studios
James Nesbitt, Larkin Werner, Bernard Uy, Doug Dean, Terrence McClusky

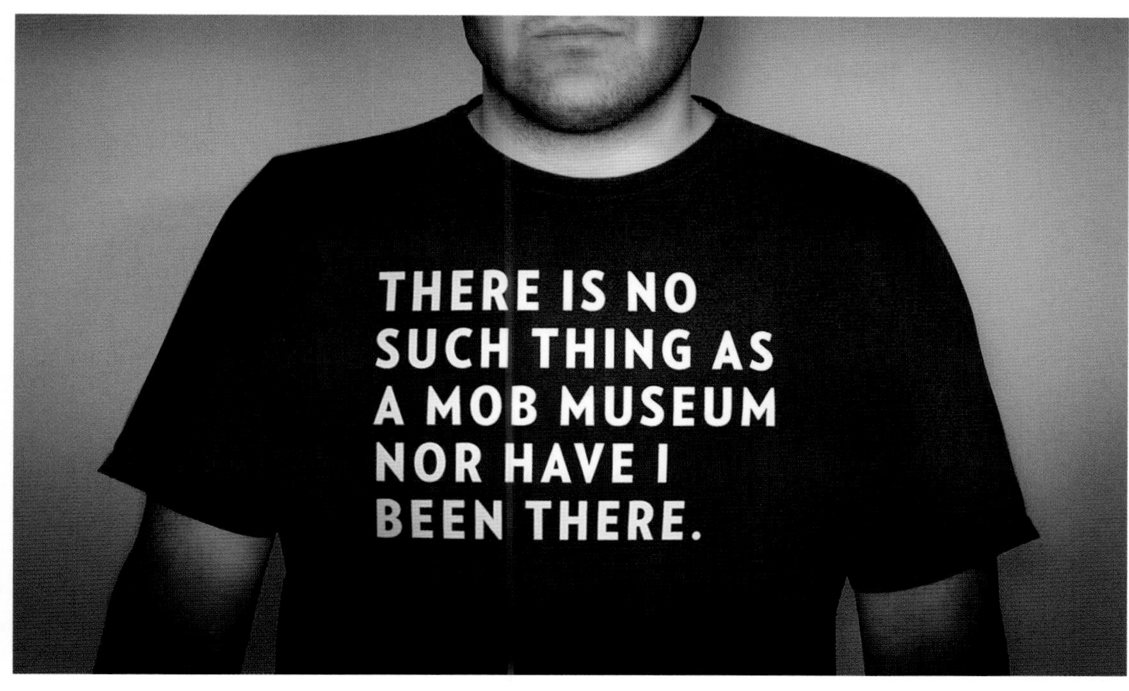

The creative team for The Mob Museum brand identity had a great idea that is funny, extendable, and memorable.

THE ~~MOB~~ MUSEUM

Las Vegas Museum of
Organized Crime
and Law Enforcement.

79 Standing for Something

The best businesses—and the best graphic identities—embody an ideal. If the founders aimed high when conceiving the business, it stands to reason to aim high when designing the mark that will represent it in the marketplace.

The graphic identity itself is often an idealized form—a geometric abstraction or other simplified version of an image. If you consider the role of symbols in daily life, they very often draw upon deep beliefs or experiences: history, nature, religion, patriotism. This isn't to say that every logo for every styling salon needs to evoke some deeper meaning, but even the ubiquitous barber pole has a rich legacy.

Logos that represent an idealized state tend to be easier to get excited about: service, quality, speed, performance, health, etc. The graphic identity becomes a symbol for the ideal solution to a customer problem.

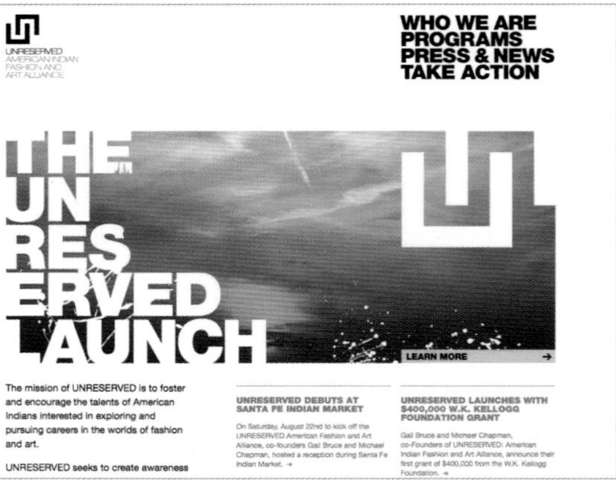

1

The website for the American Indian Fashion and Art Alliance straddles two cultures.

1. Unreserved: American Indian Fashion and Art Alliance
The O Group
Jason B. Cohen,
J. Kenneth Rothermich

2. NYC 2012
BIG/Ogilvy
Brian Collins, Bill Darling, Charles Hall, Bobby Martin, Leigh Okies, Charles Watlington, Robert Giampietro, Kevin Smith

2

The NYC 2012 Olympic campaign had an understandable sense of gravity or importance.

80 Building toward Something

Identity program designers orchestrate many small steps to help deliver on the promise of an ideal. The mark itself symbolizes the ideal, but everyday artifacts, spaces, services, or other interactions may add or detract from the promise of that ideal.

The customer problem—what a brand should aim to solve—is often felt in small pain points over time. Brands promise to deliver an ideal solution to the customer problem. A well-designed system of program elements builds upon itself to reflect, extend, interpret, and continuously strive to reach the ideal.

Program elements for Frank, the restaurant at the Frank Gehry-designed Art Gallery of Ontario, builds on the architect's reputation and design sensibilities.

Frank at the AGO
Hahn Smith Design
Nigel Smith, Alison Hahn, Richard Marazzi, Fred Tan, Emily Fung

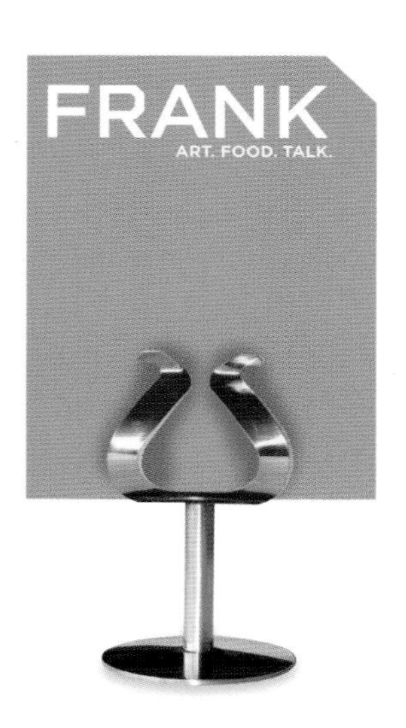

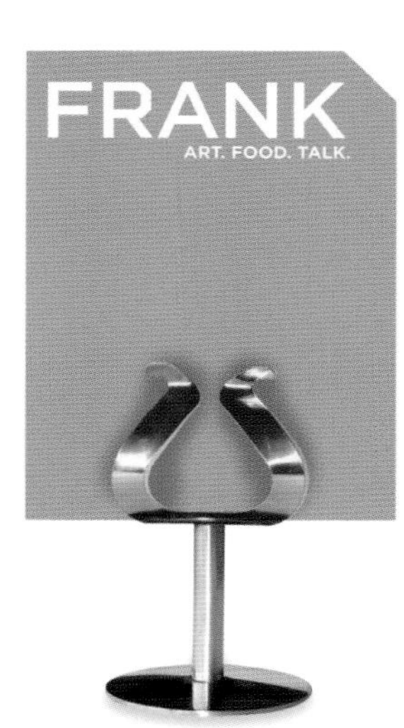

ANYTHING YOU BUILD ON A LARGE SCALE OR WITH INTENSE PASSION INVITES CHAOS.
Francis Ford Coppola, Director

81 Promising Something

There is a reason positioning templates are structured to force an organization to consider what they are going to be the best at: Are they going to be the cheapest? The coolest? The smartest? The easiest? These are simple paradigms well understood by customers, making ownership in one of these areas worth seeking.

Brand identities are built on such paradigms. The value proposition doesn't need to be all about superlatives per se, but people do seek ideals in their daily lives. Meaningful brands align their offering with customer needs, emphasizing their solution as the best.

Many businesses will require healthy doses of pragmatism as well, but unless the ideal customers are striving for is to be the most pragmatic (which is unlikely), pragmatism should not find its way into the brand identity. There are casualties in every conflict, and building a strong brand requires isolating the ideals represented by the team's flag.

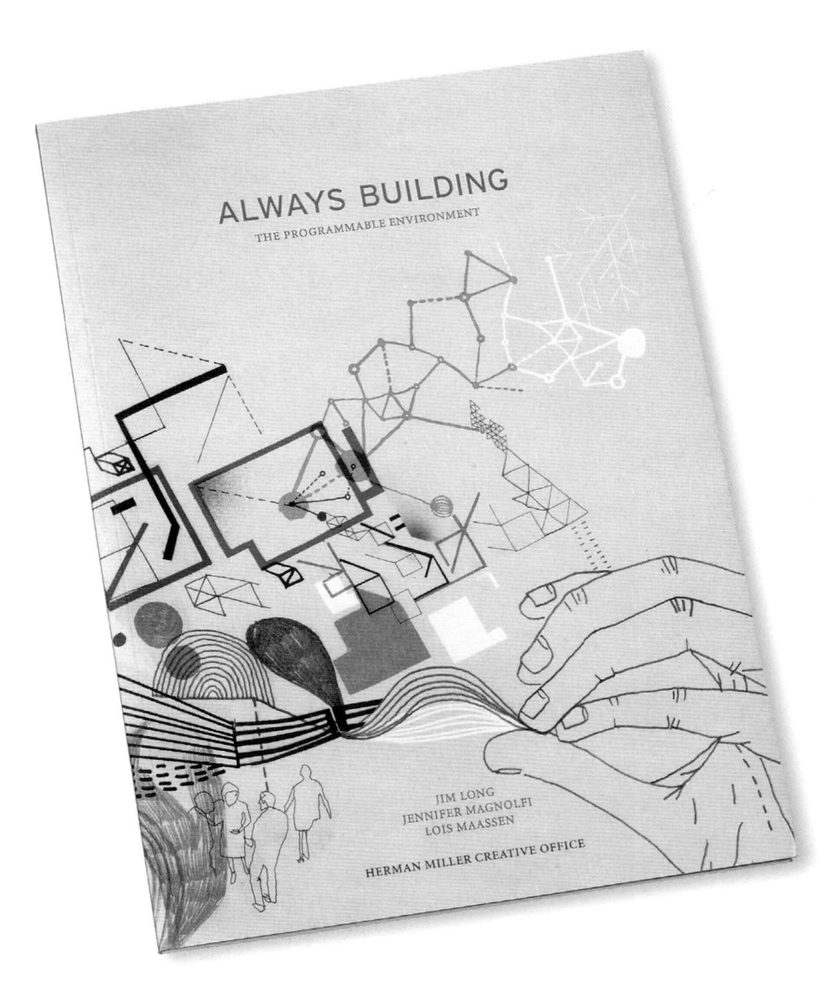

Brands worth following strive for an idealized state that is well understood and valued by customers. For its *Always Building* book, Herman Miller wanted to inspire a sense of possibility about the evolved workplace.

Herman Miller *Always Building*
People Design

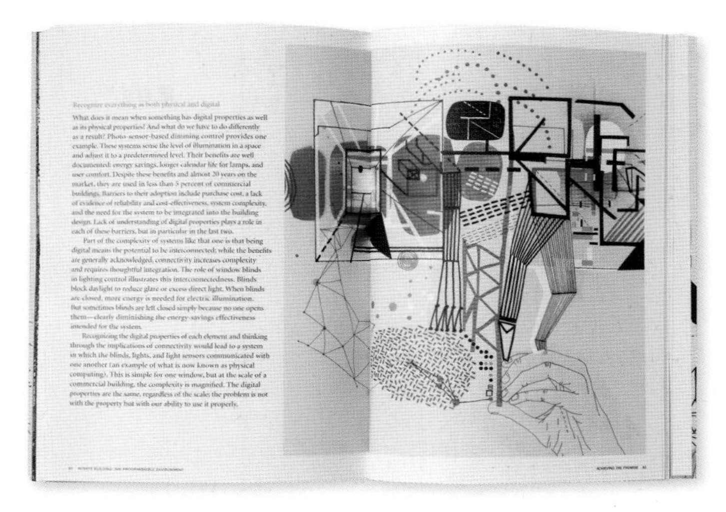

Recognize everything as both physical and digital

What does it mean when something has digital properties as well as its physical properties? And what do we have to do differently as a result? Photo-sensor-based dimming control provides one example. These systems sense the level of illumination in a space and adjust it to a predetermined level. Their benefits are well documented: energy savings, longer calendar life for lamps, and user comfort. Despite these benefits and almost 20 years on the market, they are used in less than 5 percent of commercial buildings. Barriers to their adoption include purchase cost, a lack of evidence of reliability and cost-effectiveness, system complexity, and the need for the system to be integrated into the building design. Lack of understanding of digital properties plays a role in each of these barriers, but in particular in the last two.

Part of the complexity of systems like that one is that being digital means the potential to be interconnected; while the benefits are generally acknowledged, connectivity increases complexity and requires thoughtful integration. The role of window blinds in lighting control illustrates this interconnectedness. Blinds block daylight to reduce glare or excess direct light. When blinds are closed, more energy is needed for electric illumination. But sometimes blinds are left closed simply because no one opens them—clearly diminishing the energy-savings effectiveness intended for the system.

Recognizing the digital properties of each element and thinking through the implications of connectivity would lead to a system in which the blinds, lights, and light sensors communicated with one another (an example of what is now known as physical computing). This is simple for one window, but at the scale of a commercial building, the complexity is magnified. The digital properties are the same, regardless of the scale; the problem is not with the property but with our ability to use it properly.

Observing the digital transformation of society teaches us a great deal. We have framed a vision of the future where information technology and distributed computing will not only permeate our work and daily experiences, but will also constitute the very makeup of our built environment. This will create tremendous opportunities for solving one of the long-standing problems in buildings as we know them—the costly and time-consuming effort required to accommodate change.

Our buildings are at odds with the notion of change. Fixed utilities, unforgiving infrastructure, rigid materials, and lack of control inhibit our ability to affect our surroundings. Buildings allow us only to be passive participants in their use. But what we require changes, and our inability to change the environment leads to its obsolescence.

The process of designing a building or interior environment is imbued with flexibility. It is a dynamic dialog between designer and artifact influenced by the requirements and values of all stakeholders. Flexibility, however, disappears once construction begins. The efficiency of construction and the economics of the overall process hinge on the design being frozen in time, casting change as an enemy of budgets and schedules. In the end, the space as built constitutes the final design. The building becomes a static expression of a set of requirements that began to change before the first occupant moved in.

New technologies can resolve the conflict between the freedom and interactivity of the design process and the static environments the process generates. It is becoming possible for buildings to change more efficiently and gracefully. Materials are becoming less rigid. Infrastructures are becoming more modular, consequently more suited for change. And control has the potential to be distributed in ways that allow design processes to become a part of the use and operation of a building.

The development and application of this technology requires innovation in all aspects of building design, construction, operation,

"We shape our buildings, and afterwards our buildings shape us."
—Winston Churchill, 1943

"We become what we behold. We shape our tools and then our tools shape us."
—Marshall McCluhan, 1964

THE PROMISE 21

Our interest is in designing, building, and using the built environment. Our particular focus is the interior spaces of buildings—how they will change, how they can be better, how they can deliver what occupants need and do so more efficiently. What we need are new ways of seeing the world and different ways of thinking about how we interact with our environments. Here are five areas of change that provide some of these perspectives. While neither comprehensive nor conclusive, they provoke new ideas and lead to different ways of thinking.

Toward efficient, sustainable construction

The global construction industry employs more than 100 million people and an annual investment estimated at $4.6 trillion. Of that, the Construction Industry Institute estimates "up to 57 percent non-value-added effort or waste"; vacant buildings and empty offices suggest underutilization. Yet the amount of commercial space continues to grow. Since 1950 the amount of commercial space per capita in the U.S. has grown from 183 to 268 square feet per person—an increase of close to 50 percent.

The costs of operating and owning a building are high, in both financial and environmental terms. Commercial buildings in the U.S. account for nearly 18 percent of energy consumption, including nearly 33 percent of all electricity. Costs compound as occupants come and go, a building's use changes, and new technologies are introduced and layered in; the building and its systems become more complex and more difficult to support and maintain.

Building obsolescence is signaled by the proliferation of "for lease" signs in our business parks, downtowns, and strip malls—while new construction goes up alongside. In the U.S. alone, nearly 50,000 commercial buildings are demolished each year, adding to nearly 150 million tons of construction and demolition waste that is difficult to reclaim or recycle.

DEMOLITION ADDS TO LANDFILL
The nearly 50,000 commercial buildings demolished each year in the U.S. produce nearly 150 million tons of construction and demolition waste each year.

"Sustainability is never a static goal. It can only be a process."
—Bruce Sterling

24 ALWAYS BUILDING: THE PROGRAMMABLE ENVIRONMENT

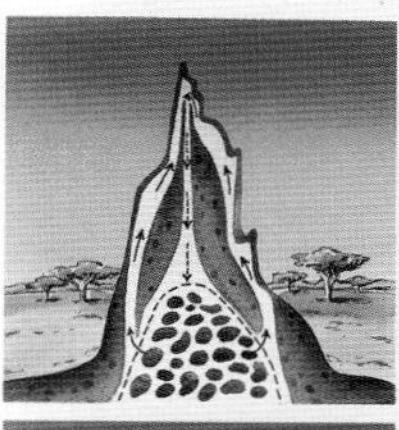

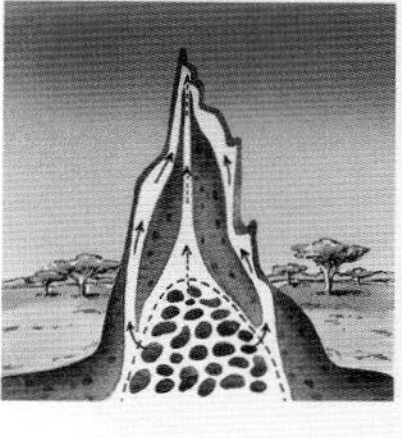

LEARNING FROM NATURE
The Eastgate Centre is cooled without conventional air conditioning through biomimicry. Termites in Zimbabwe open and close ventilation passages throughout the day, using convection currents to keep the interior of their enormous mounds at a constant temperature. Breezes are directed into the cool mud below the mound during the heat of the day; those passages are closed at night to preserve the heat retained in the mound. The Eastgate Centre reinterprets the same principles through its application of vents, ducts, exhaust ports, and chimneys.

THE PROMISE 25

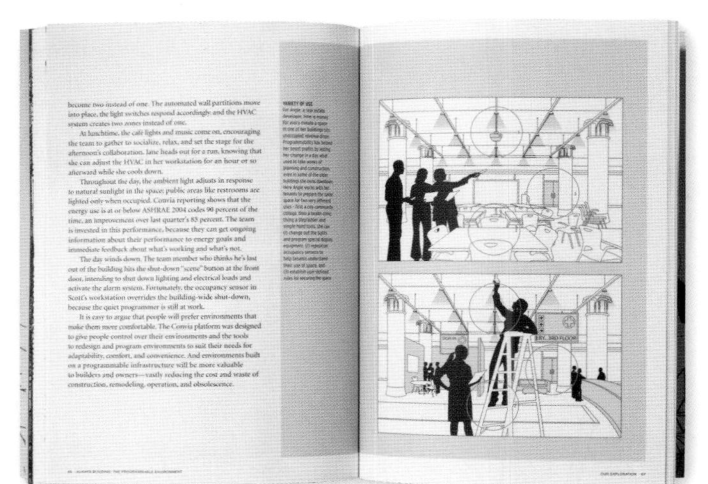

become two instead of one. The automated wall partitions move into place, the light switches respond accordingly and the HVAC system creates two zones instead of one.

At lunchtime, the café lights and music come on, encouraging the team to gather to socialize, relax, and set the stage for the afternoon's collaboration. Jane heads out for a run, knowing that she can adjust the HVAC in her workstation for an hour or so afterward while she cools down.

Throughout the day, the ambient light adjusts in response to natural sunlight in the space; public areas like restrooms are lighted only when occupied. Convia reporting shows that the energy use is at or below ASHRAE 2004 codes 90 percent of the time, an improvement over last quarter's 85 percent. The team is invested in this performance, because they can get ongoing information about their performance to energy goals and immediate feedback about what's working and what's not.

The day winds down. The team member who thinks he's last out of the building hits the shut-down "scene" button at the front door, intending to shut down lighting and electrical loads and activate the alarm system. Fortunately, the occupancy sensor in Scott's workstation overrides the building-wide shut-down, because the quiet programmer is still at work.

It is easy to argue that people will prefer environments that make them more comfortable. The Convia platform was designed to give people control over their environments and the tools to redesign and program environments to suit their needs for adaptability, comfort, and convenience. And environments built on a programmable infrastructure will be more valuable to builders and owners—vastly reducing the cost and waste of construction, remodeling, operation, and obsolescence.

VARIETY OF USE

The Herman Miller Creative Office didn't set out to pursue programmable environments. We recognized the same societal forces as did many of our research colleagues in other organizations. We had some biases and beliefs—specifically, that people and their experiences are important and often don't get the attention they should. That environmental sustainability is, as it's now widely recognized, one of the leading issues for current generations to address on behalf of future generations. That the infusion of technology into every aspect of our lives both is inevitable and offers enormous potential for good. And, of course, given the longstanding focus of Herman Miller's research and innovation, that the built environment is worthy of investment as both a reflection and an enabler of human endeavor.

Our charter was to identify ways to create value for all of the parties involved in built environments—those who build them, maintain them, manage them, furnish them, and use them. We scouted many different areas—innovations in solid state lighting, the interaction of wearable computing with environments, design informatics, DC electrical distribution, indoor air quality, flexible ducts, and environmentally powered sensors. We generally kept these explorations separate. But the more we explored, the more we saw value in the connections between things that are not, in conventional practices, connected. We found possibilities like:

- Using lighting technology and new textile technology as a way to define adaptive space
- Integrating lighting, audio, and display capabilities into space-making elements
- Finding ways to collect building-use data and integrate the data into renovation projects
- Designing single systems for utility delivery—that combine, for example, electricity and communication for control
- Activating ceiling elements, generally simple covers for plenum spaces, to create temporary dedicated-use spaces

EXPERIMENTS IN FORM

82 The Truth Comes Out

Logos that try too hard, feel forced, or seem to be a stretch can stand out—in a bad way. Potential customers can spot a brand that's overpromising from a mile away.

Still, many organizations mistakenly undertake a graphic identity overhaul as a quick and easy way to upgrade their brand image. In the short term, updating a graphic identity can make an impact. A new logo certainly can imply a new or better value proposition, but a new face doesn't make a new person. Customers will expect to see a brand live up to its updated logo in the long run. Disappointing them may make the hard work of rebuilding a brand image even harder.

Organizations that are truthful in their business positioning and authentic in their brand pursuits neither undersell nor oversell the products and services they offer. For these organizations, a logo is more than a decoration. It's their flag, their company crest, their reason for getting out of bed in the morning. The rewards greatly outweigh the inherent challenges when designing graphic identities for these organizations.

Bissinger's
TOKY Branding + Design
Eric Thoelke, Jamie Banks-George, Geoff Story

Some graphic identities just seem to ring true. Do you doubt the ultra richness of Bissinger's frosting? Are you uncertain about what Schmidty's is all about?

Schmidty's
Imagehaus
Jay Miller

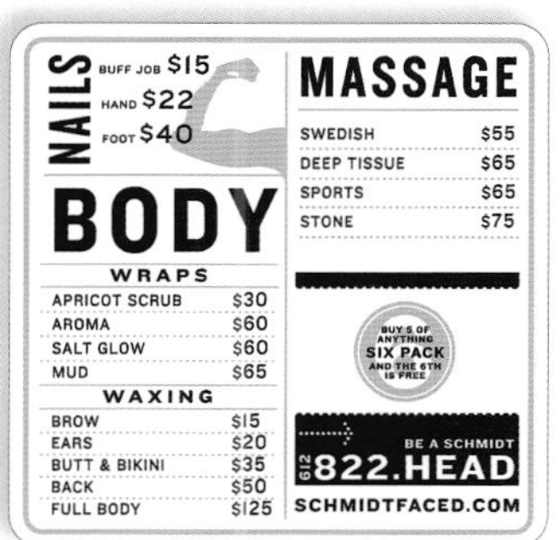

83 Authenticity Grows

Authentic brands are built day by day. Program materials are the bricks, and standards are the mortar. Be intentional when considering these materials, and be consistent when executing them.

More often than not, a lot of little things add up to an authentic brand. Any provider can make a claim about on-time service, but only those that deliver on such claims day in and day out are being authentic. An authentic brand message might acknowledge an organization's effort rather than puffing up performance claims.

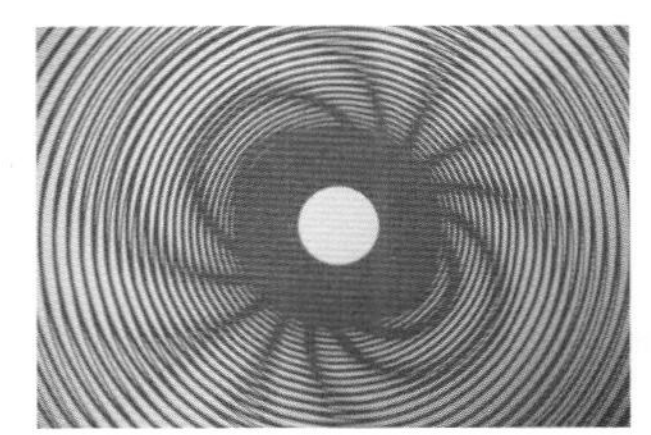

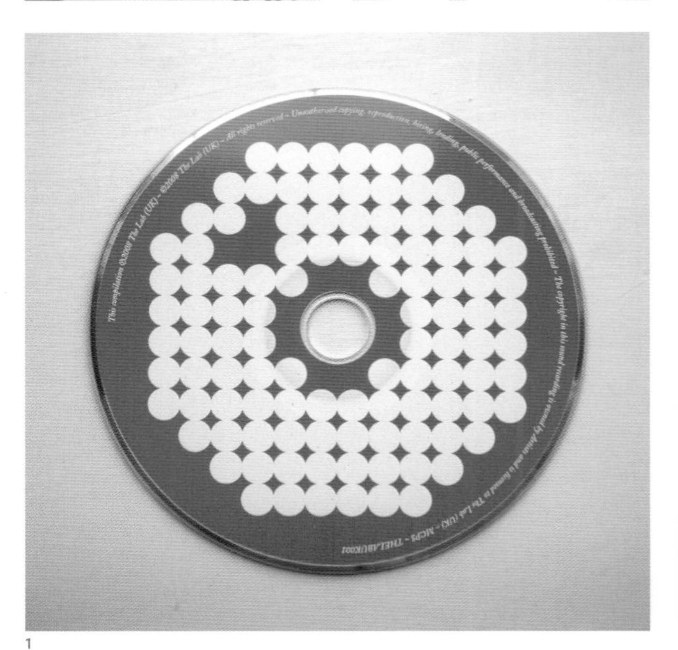

1

1. The Lab
G-MAN

2. Flora Grubb Gardens
Volume Inc.
Adam Brodsley,
Eric Heiman, Amber Reed,
Marcelo Viana

I'm Saul Nadler

Swing by our garden at 1634 Jerrold Ave.
San Francisco, California 94124.
Ring me at 415 694 6440 or call the store
at 415 648 2670. Fax us at 415 648 0777 or
drop me a line at saul@floragrubb.com.

I'm Laura Stratton

Swing by our garden at 1634 Jerrold Ave.
San Francisco, California 94124.
Ring me at 415 694 6453 or call the store
at 415 648 2670. Fax us at 415 648 2674 or
drop me a line at laura@floragrubb.com.

A little thing like follow-through goes a long way in developing program materials for an authentic brand. For The Lab and Flora Grubb Gardens, every piece adds up.

2

84 Honesty Is Sustainable

Authenticity speaks volumes. Brands that tell a genuine, honest story resonate with people. People believe in honest brands.

Even if you don't think people can spot a fake intuitively, the digital age has given rise to a new era of transparency. Twitter, blogs, and twenty-four-hour news cycles are forcing companies to live up to their promises more than ever. Even the most carefully crafted press release can't compete with a thousand people trashing a brand in the blogosphere.

The Internet generation values authenticity above many other brand attributes, which pushes smart brands to be real with their customers. The payoff (besides good karma) is that while today's consumers will not tolerate dishonest claims, they are more forgiving of honest mistakes.

3 Characteristics of Authentic Brands

SOURCE
Chuck Saylor
Chairman and CEO,
izzy+
izzyplus.com

Chuck Saylor founded the office furniture company known as izzy in 2001—not an ideal time to start a business in the U.S., if you recall. Yet, the company has not only survived, it has enjoyed tremendous growth, including the acquisition in 2008 of Jami Inc. and its four furniture brands (Harter, Fixtures Furniture, Zoom Seating, and ABCO Office Furniture).

Transitioning from an individual furniture brand to a house of brands presented a major challenge for izzy. The same belief in authenticity that nurtured izzy's growth has also helped guide the brand through this transition. According to Saylor, it comes down to clarity of message, courage, and follow-through.

1. Clarity of the message
And if there's meaning and purpose embedded in the message, it's even better. "When I look at a logo and the products or services it represents," Saylor said, "it all needs to sync up to a message that as a customer, I'm absolutely connected to, believe in, and want to support. It's pretty amazing how few brands reach that level."

2. Courage
Being real is far from easy—especially in an age of transparency. Once authenticity is an expressed goal for a brand, it has to permeate the organization at every level. "When you decide to be authentic, it goes way beyond the design of a logo," Saylor said. "You have to put so much of your heart and soul into it, there is great sacrifice at all levels of a business."

3. Follow-through
Once you decide to create that authentic idea, you have to sweat the small stuff. "Authenticity rings with attention to detail," Saylor said. "Every little thing matters when you're talking about authenticity."

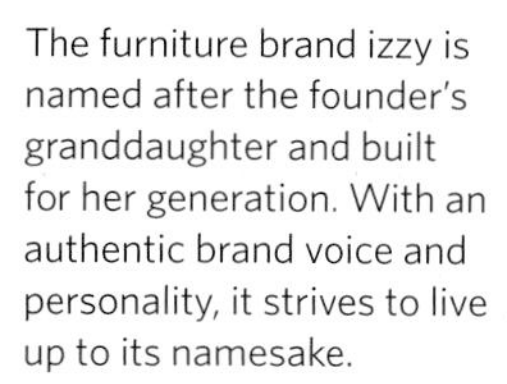

The furniture brand izzy is named after the founder's granddaughter and built for her generation. With an authentic brand voice and personality, it strives to live up to its namesake.

izzy
People Design

85 Stick with a Good Idea

Too often, a logo change is seen as a cosmetic, tactical choice, equated to changing out business cards. There can be a sense that either "we can change it later if we don't like it," or worse, that it generally doesn't matter much. Neither is accurate.

Aside from the fact that a graphic identity can be very expensive to change (the production costs alone add up quickly), this way of thinking reveals a bigger problem. A graphic identity is a foundational element of establishing the promise of a brand in the minds of its customers. Changing a logo signals a change in the brand promise, and changing it on a whim risks eroding brand equity.

A graphic identity is one of the most valuable assets of a brand—the symbolic face of the company. Once an appropriate graphic identity is established for an organization, the organization needs to commit to it. Change is inevitable. Businesses must evolve with their customers, but the most successful businesses evolve strategically.

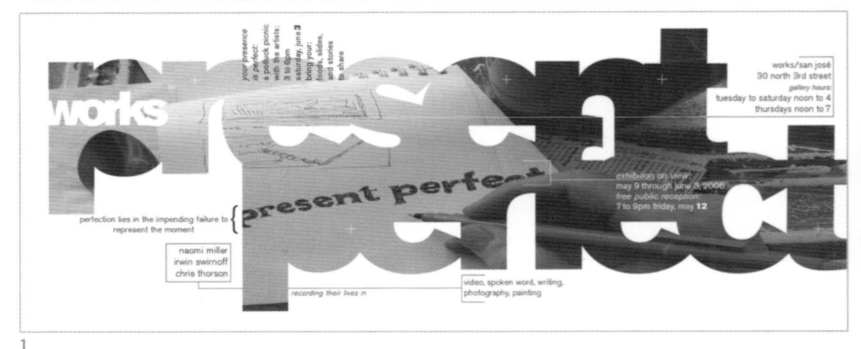

1

Both Poetry Center San José and the Star of Bethnal Green rely on spirited, dynamic graphics across their identity programs.

1. Works/San José
joe miller's company
Joe Miller

2. The Star of Bethnal Green
Bunch

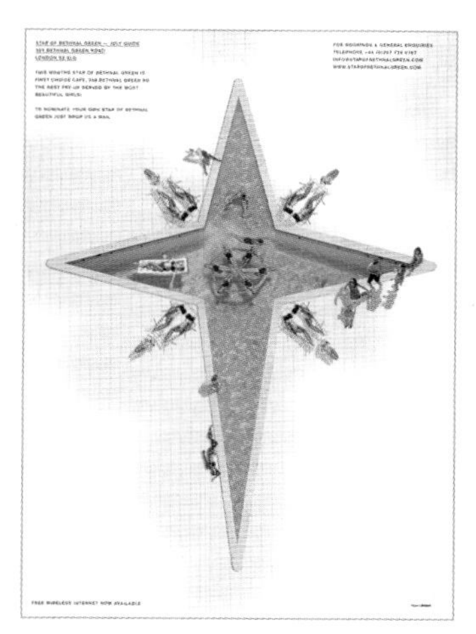

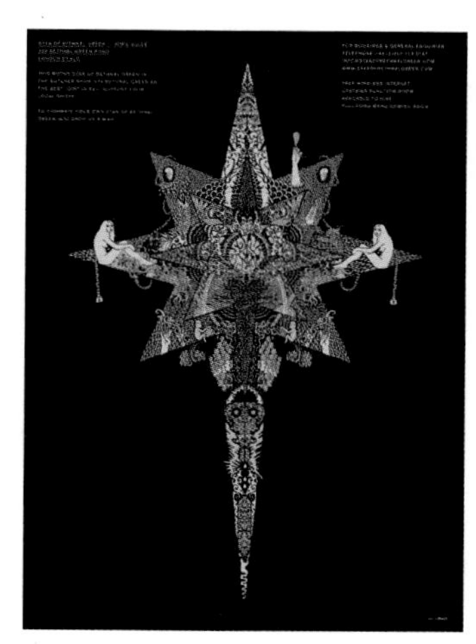

STAR
BETNAL
1st
birthday

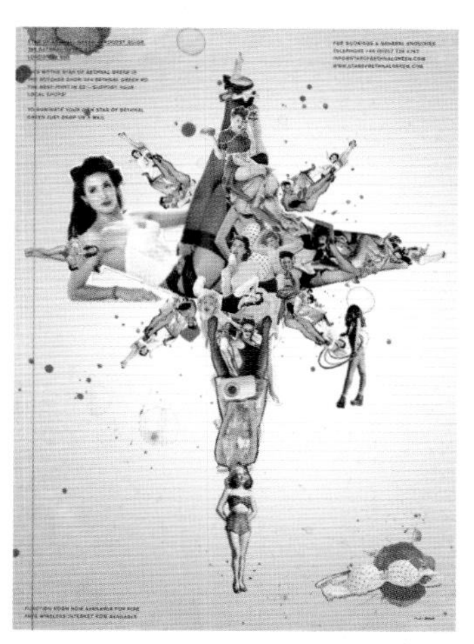

star of bethnal green – january guide
359 bethnal green road
london e2 6lg
this months star of bethnal green
is e.pellici, 332 bethnal green road
rip nevio pellici 1925 – 2008
to nominate your own star of bethnal
green just drop us a mail
for bookings + general enquiries
telephone +44 0 207 729 0167
info@starofbethnalgreen.com
www.starofbethnalgreen.com
free wireless internet
upstairs function room
available for hire
full food menu coming soon
free entry all night
every friday in januar

2

86 Program Confidence

Successful identity programs rely heavily on consistency. Consistency is a measure of confidence. Confident companies that commit to strong identity programs will see the best return on their investment. However, identity programs can have a shorter lifespan than graphic identities.

While a strategically focused organization might consider changing only its graphic identity once in a generation, programs may need to be refreshed after a three-year business cycle. Program variations might be necessitated by events—campaigns, trade shows, changing seasons—or ad hoc. Strong identity programs allow for a good balance between ordered consistency and opportunistic variation.

Confident decision makers who are willing to commit to certain brand ideals see application standards not as a limitation but as a reflection of their commitment. Designers see this commitment as another kind of constraint—and as a source of inspiration for creative problem solving.

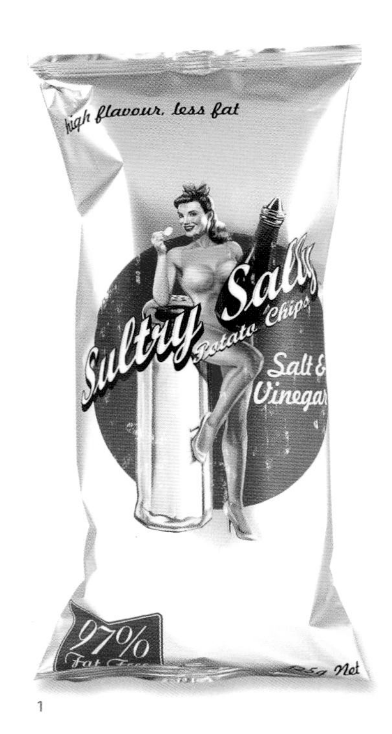

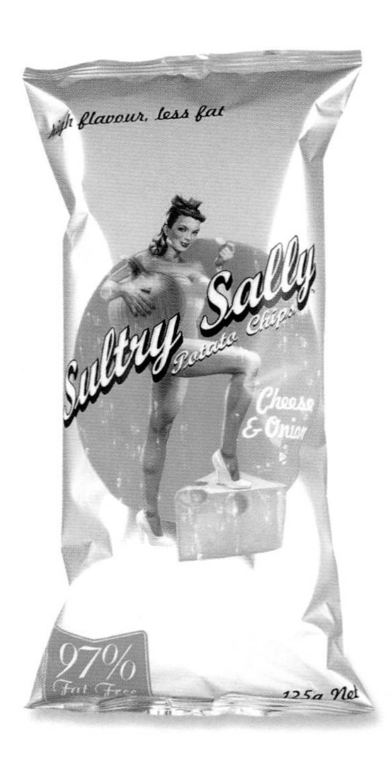

1

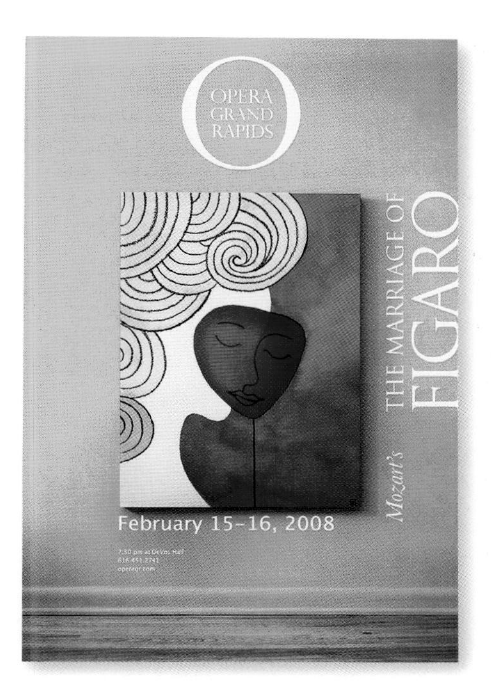

2

Sultry Sally chip bags exhibit the courage of their convictions. Each season presents Opera Grand Rapids with an opportunity to renew its commitment to its program aesthetic.

1. Sultry Sally
The Creative Method
Tony Ibbotson

2. Opera Grand Rapids
Square One Design
Lisa Dingman, Mike Gorman, Yolanda Gonzales, Sarah Mieras

87 Decisive Brands

Decision by indecision is no way to build brand value. When companies commit to a value proposition, audience, and position, they create opportunities for a strong brand identity to grow. Failure to commit is one of the most common ways to weaken a brand.

In many ways, brands are like people. People whose actions are consistent build a strong identity. They become known by the reliability of their actions—their commitments. Brands are built or torn down based on their willingness to commit and their ability to follow through.

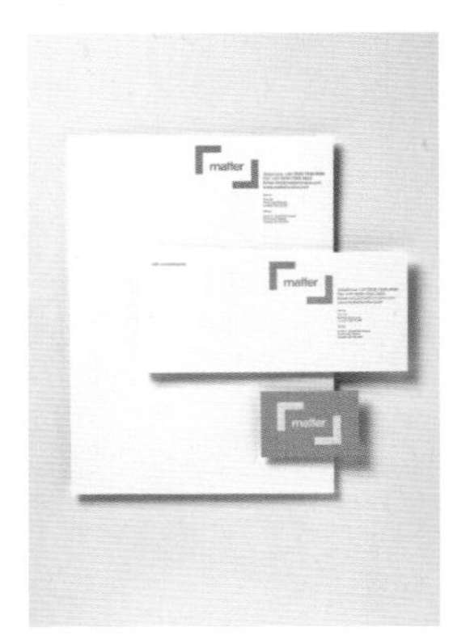

The Matter live music venue owns brackets. Throughout the program materials, things that "matter" are captured inside brackets.

matter: Interior Design
Pentagram
William Russell, Sarah Adams, Tiziana Falchi, Ali Tabrizi, Dave Perry

The identity system for Domo went all-in on a bold, distinctive direction. Once you commit to having striped pets in your logo, there's no going back—so why not have fun with them?

Domo
Brandient
Cristian "Kit" Paul, Alin Tamasan, Eugen Erhan

88 The Sign of a Promise

Strategy plays a vital role in identity design. Business strategy, marketing strategy, and communications strategy not only direct identity work, they often inspire it.

A great logo embodies the spirit of the strategic brand promise. The type of business or name can be helpful threads to follow as identity designers work to express what makes the company unique.

Good graphic identities, like good strategies, stand the test of time. A company that changes its logo frequently reflects a lack of commitment in the boardroom. Firms that understand the value in building brand equity, starting with a logo, recognize their graphic identity as a strategic choice and an important investment.

The global reach of Umbra Ltd. ArtPrize's tipped Calder. L'Abbaye College's regal mark. The seed of discovery planted in the logo of second-hand furniture store Neufundland. Cucu Land's "Be pure, be free" message. Each of these marks reflect their respective brand promises.

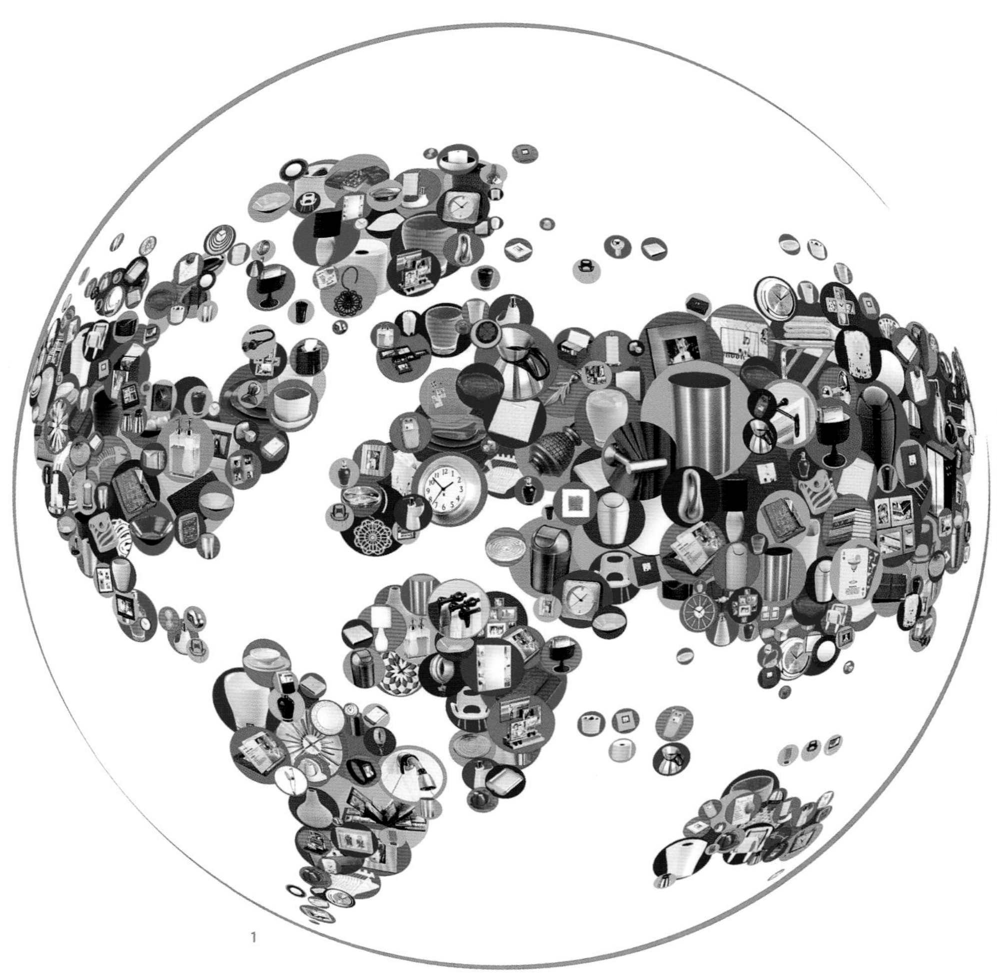

1

1. Umbra Ltd.
42ink Design
Paul Rowan, Kirstin Thomas, Chris Barnes

2. ArtPrize
People Design

3. L'Abbaye College
Wink
Richard Boynton, Scott Thares, Dan Mackaman

4. NEUFUNDLAND
Simon & Goetz Design GmbH & Co. KG
Dörte Fischer, Julia Brett, Heiko Winter

5. Cuculand
Brandient
Cristian "Kit" Paul, Cristian Petre, Bogdan Dumitrache, Eugen Erhan, Ciprian Badalan, Ianca Barbarosa

2

3

4

5

89 Customer Immersion

Marketing and communications strategies inform the tactics that make up most identity programs. A deep understanding of audience needs and goals is the basis for this work. As designers develop program components, the right mix of media, products, services, and information works together to meet the needs of this audience and help them achieve their goals. Immersing the audience in an identity program requires sound planning and perseverance.

The New Museum of Contemporary Art program materials employ various media channels.

New Museum
Wolff Olins
Jordan Crane, Jin Lee, Droga5, Lily Williams, Beth Kovalsky, Kris Pelletier, Brian Boylan, Susie Ivelich, Melissa Bamber, Erin Nolan

RP0335_1745.tif

90 Positioning

Too often, organizations see positioning as a linguistic exercise. But the perfectly worded positioning statement should not become a pursuit on par with the quest for the Holy Grail. Developing positioning and writing a mission statement are two different exercises. While spending time carefully crafting the appropriate mission statement is well worth doing, it should be done later.

Positioning—whether it's for products or companies—is a strategic exercise. Useful models developed by the Harvard Business School, Kellogg School of Management, and other credible sources are readily available. These simple templates demystify the strategic positioning exercise.

Positioning is all about making tough choices. Being all things to all people is not a strategic position. Something's got to go. An effective brand identity requires clearly identifying whom the target audience is for the brand, what the brand's primary differentiator is, and how that claim is justified.

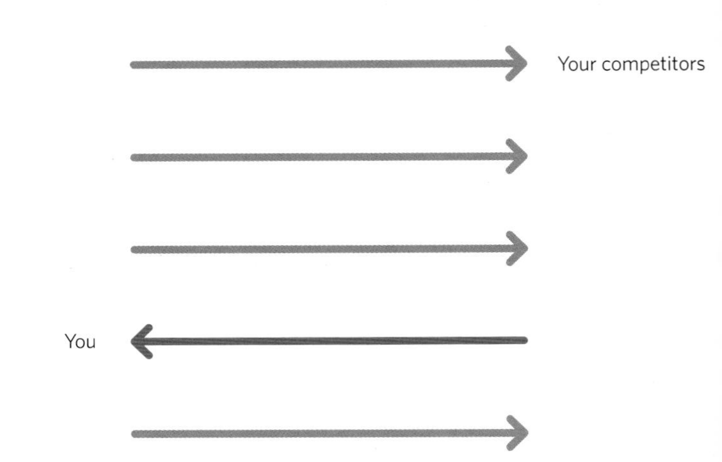

Positioning is not about changing what a company says; it's about committing to a clear direction that distinguishes a company from its competition.

Positioning diagram
Courtesy: People Design

Positioning template
Courtesy: Marty Neumeier

OUR offering IS THE ONLY category THAT benefit .

Too often, companies get distracted by the elusive mission statement. This simplified positioning template addresses the key issues required in developing a clear strategic position.

91 Do Your Homework

Before you begin designing a logo, do your homework. Some initial research can save time, and it might just be the creative spark you need to create a powerful graphic identity.

For starters, get to know the company—its current strategy and any past graphic identities that had been developed previously. The desire to be perceived as fresh or new often prompts companies to leave a rich visual history in the drawer. Mining these resources for source material provides a logical starting point for a new graphic identity.

Learn about the company's target audience: What are their needs, their preferences, and their goals? Developing a graphic identity a company's employees feel good about wearing on a T-shirt or baseball cap is an accomplishment. Identity work rooted in an understanding of the audience can transform a logo into a badge customers will proudly wear.

Additionally, find out what competitors are doing. The Internet makes it easy to conduct a quick survey of logos within the same or related categories. It's also wise to look at marks developed for companies with similar names or letterforms. Even if these other solutions do not raise a legal conflict, they're good input for your work.

Some research is best done in the field; other projects can benefit from knowledge gleaned from focus groups.

ServiceSource Workshop
C2
Erik Cox, Greg Galle, John Bielenberg

92 Constraints and Opportunities

Initial research provides a better understanding of the constraints under which an identity program will operate. Constraints may eliminate some options, but in doing so, they help define the design problem. Embrace constraints as opportunities for innovation.

Designers are well served to experience the context directly to better shape their understanding of what solution might be optimal. Find out everything you can: What is the resolution of the device? What are the color limitations of the output method? Are sound and motion options? Can it be interactive? What are the lighting conditions? Does it need to hold up to daily use?

Most media do at least one thing well, so let your insights guide you to applications that leverage the strengths of your materials. Good identity programs work across multiple media, so there may be a time and a place for everything.

Working through program constraints can be a difficult but valuable process for design innovation.

The Mob Museum Workshop
Wall-to-Wall Studios

93 Know Your Customer

Great brand identities forge a real and direct emotional connection with their customers. It starts with a deep understanding of your target audience. Needs, preferences, goals, desires: You can never know enough about your customer.

There are a wide variety of traditional customer research techniques—surveys, focus groups, etc.—but newer ethnographic research methods are becoming an increasingly larger part of the design research mix.

Ethnographic research methods are aimed at discovering unmet or unarticulated customer needs that are less likely to be revealed with more overt research methods. They include activities such as customer observation and shadowing. Meeting the needs of customers in ways that others either currently don't or can't is a true competitive advantage.

You are not your customer. The Siegel+Gale team realized that when they developed the identity program for Word World, which is targeted at a specific demographic—kids—and designed accordingly.

Word World
Siegel+Gale
Douglas Sellers, Joo Chae

Where words come alive.™
WordWorld

This is the story of how WordWorld™ opens the world of reading to the world of kids.

When they enter WordWorld™, children discover they can play with letters to build words – words they set free to become things, objects, friends and playmates.

By cleverly and uniquely connecting letters to form words and words to form things.

WordWorld™ is an exciting, fun, new way for kids to learn pre-literacy skills.

Word World™
Where words come alive™

94 Experiencing the Logo

A great way to design a holistic brand experience it to consider all customer touchpoints—the places the brand touches the customer.

The best graphic identities translate well to a variety of customer touchpoints. Large firms with literally thousands of touchpoints require the most flexible graphic identities. The brand image must be preserved as the logo is applied to everything from paper cups to ocean liners. Smaller firms may not have as many requirements, but the same logic applies—even the smallest business has invoices and a website, and these touchpoints merit consideration.

Production techniques, graphic standards, and a right-sized plan are worth some upfront investment to ensure each touchpoint expresses the graphic identity as intended. It's not only protecting an investment, but the entry point through which people experience a brand.

A logo might have more everyday customer exposure on a button than on a brochure. Make sure it works well in all touchpoints.

Film Festival EKOFILM
vgrafik
Vera Maresova, Lukas Veverka, Jakub Sporek

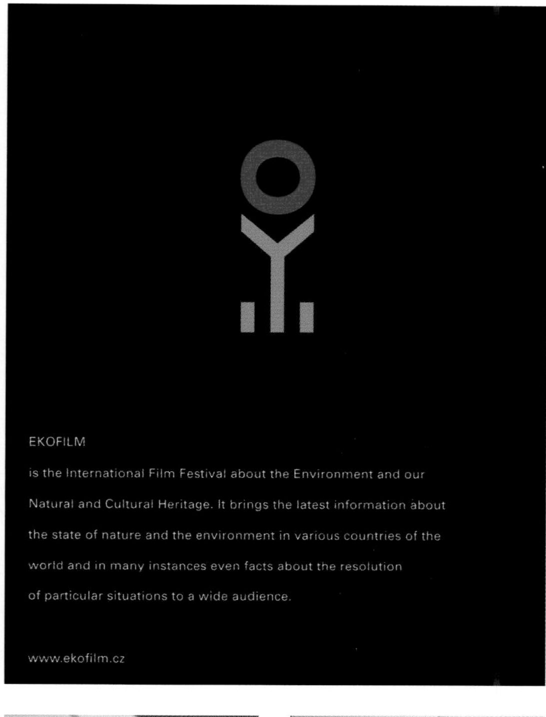

EKOFILM

is the International Film Festival about the Environment and our Natural and Cultural Heritage. It brings the latest information about the state of nature and the environment in various countries of the world and in many instances even facts about the resolution of particular situations to a wide audience.

www.ekofilm.cz

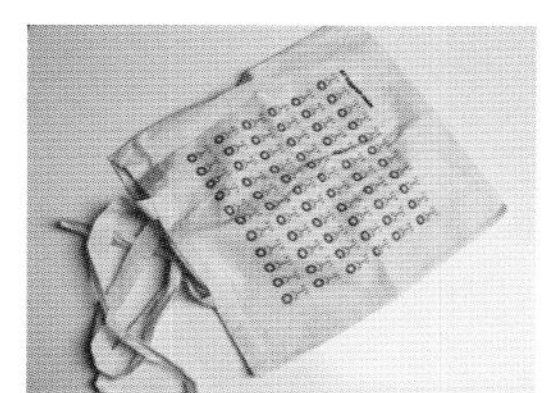

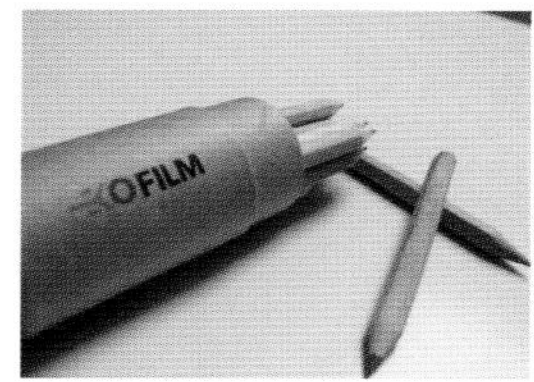

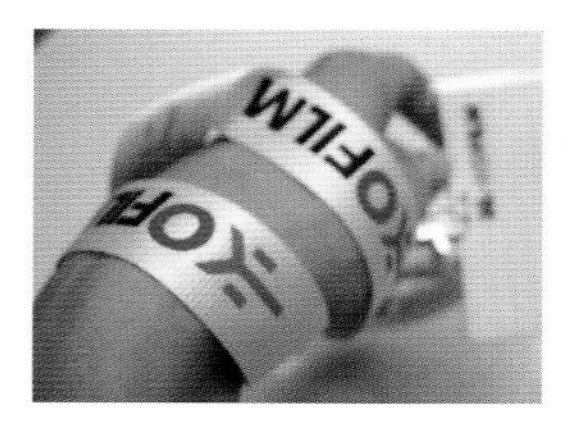

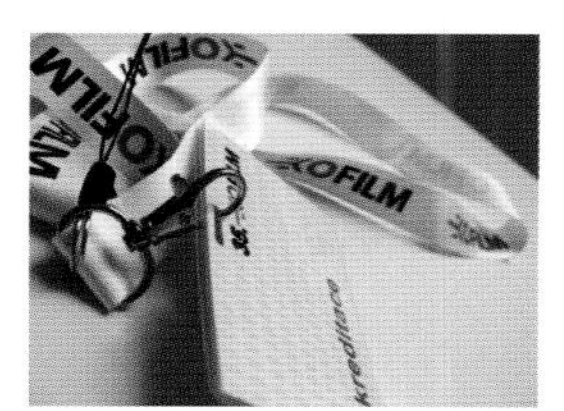

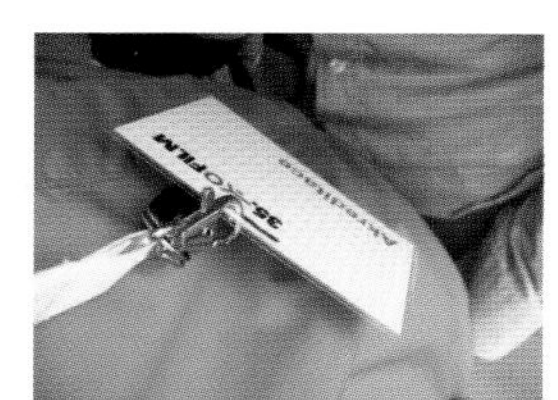

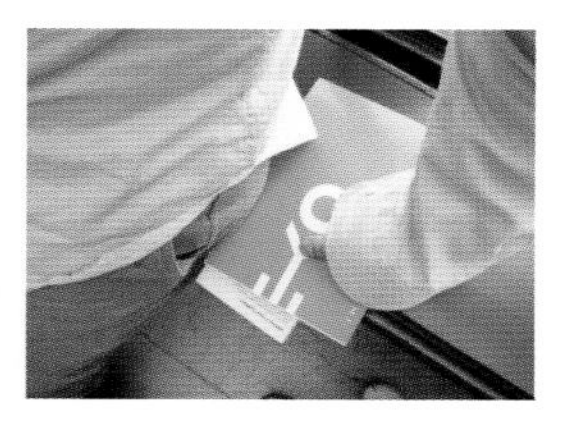

95 Connecting the Dots

Touchpoint planning is about connecting the dots before a customer experiences your brand. As such the exercise is a key part of designing strong identity programs.

Not all touchpoints are the same, nor do they have equal value. Some touchpoints happen almost all at once and, therefore, require greater continuity than those that exist separately. Some touchpoints occur regularly, which implies a kind of rhythm, while others are ad hoc, providing a little splash or surprise. Some touchpoints may go overlooked by customers, while others directly influence their buying decision.

Graphic identities can extend into many touchpoints in the customer experience.

1. American Numismatic Society
Piscatello Design Centre
Rocco Piscatello, Junno Hamaguchi

2. HTZ/Croatian National Tourist Board
STUDIO INTERNATIONAL
Boris Ljubicic

3. Community Foundation of Greater Chattanooga
Maycreate
Brian May, Monty Wyne, Chris Enter

4. Gourmet Settings
Hahn Smith Design
Nigel Smith, Alison Hahn

5. amala
Liska + Associates
Tanya Quick, Jenn Cash

6. Ila
Pentagram
John Rushworth

7. No Frizz by Living Proof
Wolff Olins
Todd Simmons, Tiziana Haug, Sung Kim, Mary Ellen Muckerman, Carmine Montalto, Beth Kovalsky, Michele Miller

8. Vertafore
Siegel+Gale
Sven Seger, Young Kim, Robert Schroeder, Lana Roulhac, Joo Chae

9. Sugoi
Nancy Wu Design
Ian Grais, Chris Staples, Nancy Wu, April Haffenden, Leanna Wilson, Joe Ramirez

10. House of Cards
Pentagram
Domenic Lippa

11. Artificio
Gabriela Soto Grant

12. Mercantile Exchange
TOKY Branding + Design
Eric Thoelke, Travis Brown

1

2

3

4

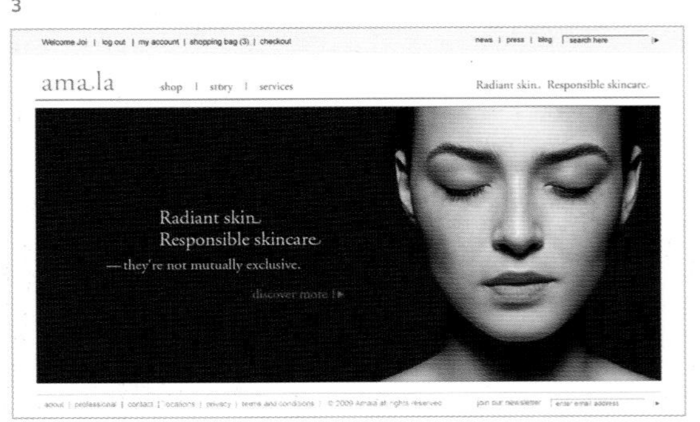

5

6

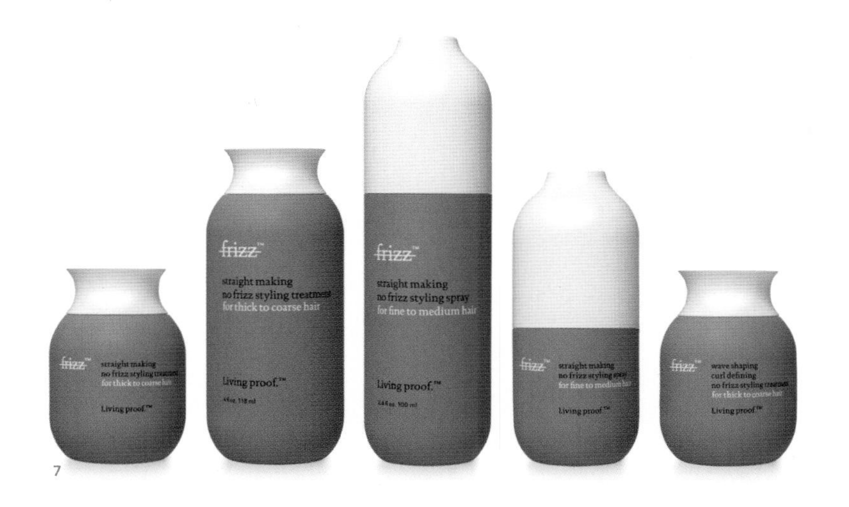

7

8

9

10

11

12

13

14

15

16

17

18

19

20

13. The Dorchester Collection
Pentagram
John Rushworth

14. BXC
BXC Inc.
Drew Dougherty, Betty Ra, Felipe Bascope

15. Rooster
TOKY Branding + Design
Eric Thoelke, Jamie Banks-George

16. Agility
Siegel+Gale
Sven Seger, Marcus Bartlett, Monica Chai, Inesa Figueroa, Holmfridur Hardardottir

17. Over the Moon
The Creative Method
Tony Ibbotson, Andi Yanto

18. Get London Reading
KentLyons
James Kent, Mark Diggins, Ric Bell, Jon Cefai, Adrian Ridley, Jon Reading

19. Yoshi's Jazz Club and Restaurant
Chen Design Associates
Joshua Chen, Laurie Carrigan, Shadi Kashefi

20. Meredith
Lippincott
Connie Birdsall, Jenifer Lecker, Shelby Brea

96 Customer Experience Planning

Customer touchpoints shape a customer's perception of a brand. These perceptions shape brand identity as much as the work of any designer or brand manager. After all, brand identity is all about what the customer thinks—not what you think. Customer perceptions are created by a series of touchpoints—the interactions customers have with a brand.

Customer experience planning is a powerful brand-management tool. It provides a framework not only for answering key questions but also for realizing better outcomes: How do customers currently experience a brand? What about competitive brands? How would you like them to experience the brand? Changing, adding, or removing touchpoints can reshape the customer's perception of your brand.

Touchpoint strategies that reflect customer needs and company positioning contribute to strong brands.

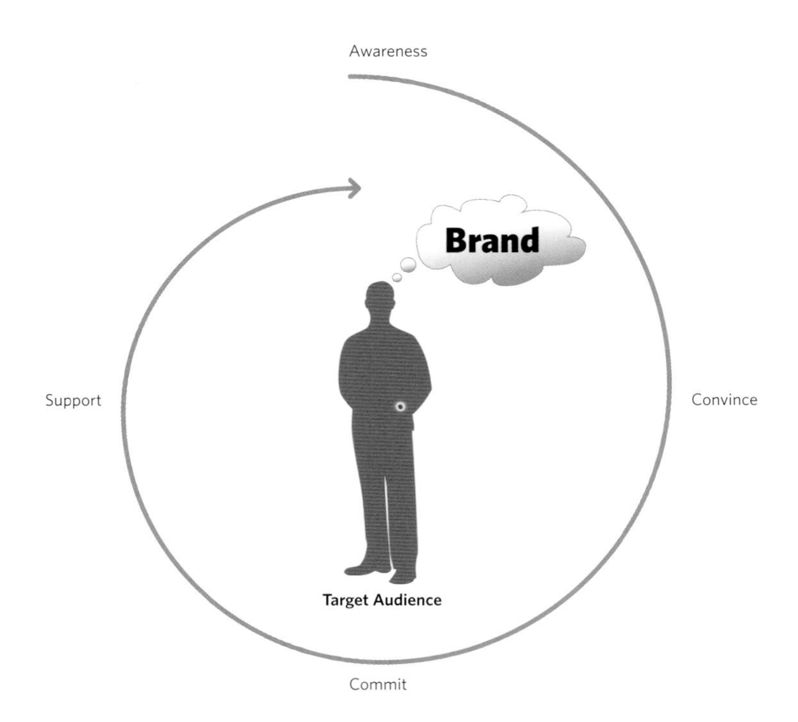

Customer Experience Map
Courtesty: People Design

3 Considerations for Customer Experience Planning

Customer experience design is the discipline of understanding customer needs, making choices about an ideal customer experience path, and creating memorable customer touchpoints that affect customer perception—or brand value.

Knowing current perception is an important first step in shaping perception. Next is the hard work of positioning, which is less about writing a statement and more about making strategic choices. Determining the target customer and finding out ways to create value for that customer will lead to an understanding of an ideal perception goal. The perception goal will guide touchpoint planning, as strategists consider touchpoints along the ideal customer path, from driving awareness to convincing to buying right on to providing support after purchase.

Once touchpoint planning is complete, media expertise, craft, and many other tools come into play as each touchpoint is realized. Each touchpoint effort should be designed in a way that is cognizant of the others, but should also stand on its own as a memorable, effective experience.

Here are a few other things to keep in mind:

1. Alignment
Each customer interaction or touchpoint either helps to build, or erodes, the perception goal. You can't not communicate.

2. Failure modes
Organizations often fail to view touchpoints as a linear progression from the customer's point of view. Too many touchpoint activities are produced to meet internal expectations and result in incongruent customer experiences.

3. Key touchpoints
Mapping all customer touchpoints may seem overwhelming, but not all touchpoints are created equal. Depending on your position, certain key touchpoints—those that are critical for keeping brand promises—are important to identify at the outset.

Touchpoint maps are a good way to plan the ideal customer experience.

Dollie & Me
Siegel+Gale
Sven Seger, Anne Swan, Kate Trogran, Ju Hyun Lee, Alex Kroll

97 A Good Idea

Where does a good idea come from? As unsexy as it might sound, many of the best ideas for graphic identities come directly from a business plan, drawing inspiration from constraints and the target audience. But clearly, the world's best graphic identities also draw upon other unseen inspirations.

Good designers draw from a variety of their life experiences—art, pop culture, children's television, etc. That's why so many designers like to be sponges when it comes to sources of inspiration. Designers should look for non-project ways of being inspired and renewed. It's not only good for mental health but also for professional development.

It's important for professional designers to not be overly committed to their personal interests—at least at work. Professional designers get paid to solve other people's problems, not chase after their own pet pursuits. At the same time, designers who become indistinguishable from businesspeople risk losing a creative edge, a competitive advantage, and the empathy that good design requires.

1

Good design is also appropriate design. Each of these graphic identities draws inspiration from the context of their respective organizations: the name "Proof" for an open-minded wine marketing firm, books for a bookstore, the Olympic rings and the sea for the Mediterranean Games, and a cityscape for the town of Kutina.

1. Mediterranean Games
Studio International
Boris Ljubicic

2. Proof Wine Marketing
Alphabet Arm Design
Aaron Belyea, Ryan Frease

3. Libreria Formatos Bookstore
Xose Teiga

4. Town of Kutina
Studio International
Boris Ljubicic, Igor Ljubicic

2

liıbreríıaformatos

3

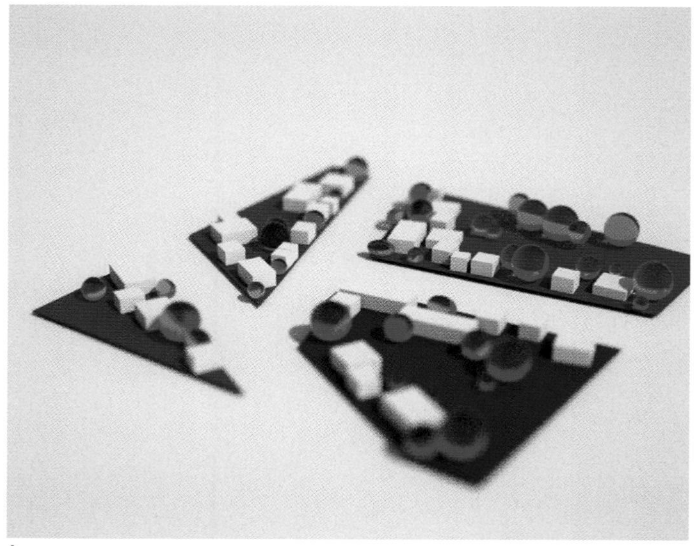

4

98 Contextual Inspiration

The inspiration behind identity programs often comes from the context of their constituent parts. Where is the identity going to be experienced? What materials or techniques might provide an inspirational/aspirational experience in that context?

Designers need to see firsthand the places where their identities are going to be applied. If you're designing a program for a grocery store, go to the store. Go a competitor's store—better yet, go to several competitors' stores. What's going on in these stores? How are people interacting with other brands? What works? What doesn't? Look for patterns. Inspired solutions often reveal themselves when you take the time to understand the context.

Sometimes, the inspiration for a program comes from one breakthrough insight about one element of the program. If an inspired approach solves one important problem really well, how might that idea be extended to other program materials? What program elements can be designed to echo or reinforce the idea? Inspired programs maintain a sense of vitality often spurred by a few simple artifacts.

Okanagan Spring
Subplot Design Inc.
Matthew Clark, Roy White, Jeff Lewis, Lana Porter Group, Clinton Hussey, Raeff Miles, Total Graphics, Rayment Collins, Rhino Print Solutions

Some of the best program ideas come from customer empathy—understanding the customer context. The craft beer drinker targeted by Okanagan Spring has an appreciation for handmade ales and natural ingredients.

99 99% Perspiration

An inspiring business plan that addresses a commonly understood human need provides the best of inspiration for a brand identity. If the brand story is clear, then the work requires translating the brand into various media and messages.

It can be difficult—though not impossible—to develop an inspired brand identity without inspired positioning. This is where marketers get a bad name. Indeed, many less than satisfactory brand experiences have been promoted with excellent campaigns. However, the smell of false advertising ultimately will rise as consumers become savvier about brand promises—and more willing to hold brands accountable when their promises are broken.

Customers increasingly look for brands that inspire them. Building a brand that delivers inspiration is hard work. The challenge lies first in determining what the customer values—which may or may not be something that can be reflected directly through a product or service. If it can, the trick becomes determining the best course of action for living up to the promise.

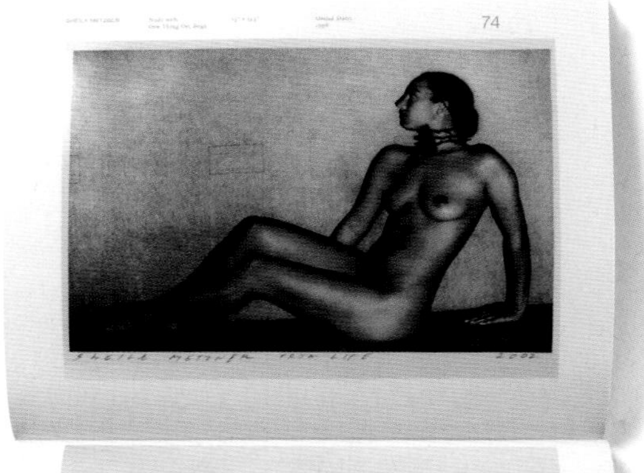

Next-generation brands will have an inspired purpose—and in turn will inspire customers. But it won't be easy.

Dove Exhibit
BIG/Ogilvy
Brian Collins, Leigh Okies, Satian Pengsathapon, David Israel

100 Keep It Simple

Simple is better.

ACKNOWLEDGMENTS

Working collaboratively can be intrinsically rewarding, but with a book project like this one, the list of people you want to thank can become unwieldy. That said, we'll do our best here to remember everyone.

First of all, we would like to thank our colleagues at People Design for their enthusiastic support of this project. Thanks, everyone, for your feedback, your flexibility, and your willingness to humor us as we wallpapered the studio with submissions for the book. Special thanks to: Andy Weber for developing brand-identity-essentials.com. Vicki Post, for tackling production design; Gina Caratelli, for taming the wall of assets. And Diana Racek, for keeping us on track through it all.

We'd also like to thank Emily Potts, David Martinell, and all the folks at Rockport Publishers. We appreciate the opportunity, and the freedom to run with it in our own way. Your patience and professionalism helped make this a better book.

We were blown away by the response we received for our call for entries, and we're grateful to all the talented designers who submitted their work for our consideration.

Thanks to our image-makers—Jeremy Frechette, Terry Johnston, Dean Van Dis, Sue Mann, and Jody Williams—for helping us in a pinch. And to those wise individuals who contributed sidebars—Mary Bonnema, Leatrice Eiseman, Bruce Hansen, and Chuck Saylor—thank you for lending your expertise to this project. We were especially honored to have had a chance to talk printing for what turned out to be one last time with our friend Bruce, who passed away a few weeks after our interview with him.

Thanks to Shelly and Sugar for giving up a few weekends with Curt so we could hit our deadlines. Finally, thanks to Bruno, Toki, and Lulu, for helping us keep things in perspective.

ABOUT PEOPLE DESIGN

People Design helps leaders transform their businesses through Brand Experience Design. For more than a decade, the firm has earned a reputation for design excellence among clients and within the design community. People Design develops insights into customer behavior and builds brands by envisioning, designing, and producing innovative customer experiences. Rooted in empathy for people, the work results in strategies that connect businesses with their customers and foster loyalty.

peopledesign.com